"At last! A mature l
delightfully honest.
tening to God and t
of the heart." Through generously making his own heart available to others, he evokes in us the desire for spiritual depth. My own soul has been nurtured. And yours will be also."

—R. PAUL STEVENS, author of *Down-to-Earth Spirituality: Encountering God in the Ordinary, Boring Stuff of Life*

"Charles Ringma's beautiful and struggling reflections are a great source of encouragement for anyone seeking to build a hermitage of the heart in daily spirituality. Maturity and applicability in faith over the long haul is a hard-won and humbled thing. Glories shine and shadows loom together in this remarkably concrete and earthy book of spiritual reflections. For practical and inspired reflections on the difficult business of the ordinary Christian life, do read this book."

—PAUL TYSON, Senior Research Fellow, University of Queensland

"Drawing from traditions as diverse as Sabbath, the Desert Fathers and Mothers, and the Franciscan way, Charles Ringma reminds us that 'the hermitage of the heart' is always accessible to those who seek deeper union with God. These different traditions are challenging and respectful of the individual, as well as safe both for beginners and those on the long journey of 'Christing'! Charles's thoughtful writing reflects his own long, open-hearted journey and gentle soul."

—GODFREY FRYAR, former Bishop of Rockhampton

"Charles Ringma's personal experience of a hermitage—his self-examination and humility before God—opens a door for all of us to enter. He understands the deep paradox that being at the service of God does not obliterate the self but enables us to be a 'healing presence in the world.' Anyone of any tradition can learn great and deep lessons from *A Fragile Hope*, and I have more than a fragile hope for the world on account of the wise and true reflections that Ringma has shared with us in this book. . . . this is the kind of book you can return to often for inspiration, courage, and most of all, hope that there is a place—the hermitage of the heart—which acknowledges our divided self of saint and sinner yet offers us the space and the grace to remember that there is always and ever the choice to be more—to be that healing presence in the world, which we need now more than ever."

—Rachael Kohn, author of *The New Believers: Re-imagining God*

"Having for years been impacted by Charles's wisdom and experience, it was with joy that I sat down to read *A Fragile Hope*. My best recommendation would be to read a chapter a day or one a week to have time to sit deeply with Charles's reflections. Charles is honest and filled with grace as he takes us on his internal journey of finding/making a hermitage of the heart. As fellow travelers, we can find many familiar landmarks that we may have already found on our own journeys. I found this encouraging, as I could often play 'join the dots' with my own spiritual pilgrimage, thus offering me sustenance on my own journey. Charles has lived an expansive life and now we experience him bringing the colorful, distinct threads back together, weaving them into one tapestry."

—Justin Duckworth, Bishop

"This book's idea of a 'hermitage of the heart' is much needed in this time of prolonged liminal space, when the global COVID pandemic has scrambled our lives and work and we all hang suspended between the familiar routines of the past and the unknown uncertainties of the future. We are being invited to know God and ourselves afresh in the thick of our everyday struggles. This book outlines and recovers for us the ancient practice of stillness, echoing especially to those of us who are Asians our own spiritual heritage: making the inner being strong enough to withstand the stresses of daily life. . . . This book situates the universal longing for inner peace within the Christian tradition. As such it is a welcome companion to those in search for a meaning to our present confusion, groping about for a foothold on which to secure a future and a hope."

—MELBA PADILLA MAGGAY, Institute for Studies in Asian Church and Culture (ISACC)

"Profound and accessible, I could not put down this book when I started reading it! I have benefited from reading other books on everyday spirituality, but this one ministered to me the most! Charles distils learnings and models creative reappropriations of divine grace for our contemporary time. Coming out of the pandemic, this spiritual tract on 'a hermitage of the heart' is one book I'd repeatedly go back to for nourishment and wisdom."

—TIMOTEO D. GENER, Chancellor and Professor of Theology, Asian Theological Seminary, Philippines

A Fragile Hope

A Fragile Hope

Cultivating a Hermitage of the Heart

CHARLES R. RINGMA

CASCADE *Books* • Eugene, Oregon

A FRAGILE HOPE
Cultivating a Hermitage of the Heart

Copyright © 2021 Charles R. Ringma. All rights reserved. Except for brief quotations in critical publications or reviews, no part of this book may be reproduced in any manner without prior written permission from the publisher. Write: Permissions, Wipf and Stock Publishers, 199 W. 8th Ave., Suite 3, Eugene, OR 97401.

Cascade Books
An Imprint of Wipf and Stock Publishers
199 W. 8th Ave., Suite 3
Eugene, OR 97401

www.wipfandstock.com

PAPERBACK ISBN: 978-1-7252-8701-3
HARDCOVER ISBN: 978-1-7252-8702-0
EBOOK ISBN: 978-1-7252-8703-7

Cataloguing-in-Publication data:

Names: Ringma, Charles R., author.
Title: A fragile hope : cultivating a hermitage of the heart / Charles R. Ringma.
Description: Eugene, OR: Cascade Books, 2021 | Includes bibliographical references.
Identifiers: ISBN 978-1-7252-8701-3 (paperback) | ISBN 978-1-7252-8702-0 (hardcover) | ISBN 978-1-7252-8703-7 (ebook)
Subjects: LCSH: Hope—Religious aspects—Christianity. | Spiritual life—Christianity. | Christian life.
Classification: BV4683 .R50 2021 (print) | BV4683 (ebook)

For

Dianna Kunce
and
Denise Easter

who have given their lives to spiritually enriching
a new generation
that knows how to seek the face of God
for the glory of God and the sake of the world

Contents

Preface xiii

Introduction xvii

1. Embracing the Unexpected 1
2. Creative Reappropriation 4
3. The Jesus Prayer 7
4. Cultivating Openness 10
5. The Invitation of the Desert Fathers and Mothers 13
6. Bothering God 17
7. Becoming 20
8. Calling 23
9. The Invitation of Celtic Spirituality 27
10. Hermitage as Place 31
11. Hidden in the Heart of the World 35
12. The Divided Self 39
13. Engaging the Ordinary 42
14. The Invitation of Benedictine Spirituality 45
15. The "Normal" Christian Life? 49
16. Discouragement 53
17. Living an Ascetic Spirituality 56
18. The Invitation of the Anabaptists 60

Contents

19. A Sabbath Spirituality 64

20. Spiritual Midwifery 67

21. The Invitation of Franciscan Spirituality 70

22. Prayer and Protest 76

23. Yearning 79

24. Identifying with Jesus 82

25. Liminality 86

26. The Invitation of Ignatian Spirituality 89

27. Life's "Curve Balls" 93

28. A Fragile Hope 97

Afterword 101

Bibliography 105

Preface

IN 2016, I TOOK off six months and spent much of that time in a hermitage on my friend's property in the Queensland bush. Some of my reflections of that time were published in 2017 in a small book entitled *Sabbath Time*.[1]

Since that time, I have returned to previous commitments, which include research and writing, teaching in Asia, and various ministry projects in my hometown of Brisbane, Australia, including working for justice. I have also returned to the challenges of aging, issues of letting go, friends dying, facing one's mortality, and, most distressingly, grappling with the increasing marginalization of the Christian faith in the Western world and the wounded condition of planet earth.

While my six months' "time out" was in no way profoundly revelatory, I have continued to reflect on that time. More importantly, I have wrestled with how such a special time can become a more normal part of one's life. In other words, can one cultivate a *hermitage of the heart*. What I mean by this is, can certain inward disciplines and spiritual practices in normal life function *as if* one is in a hermitage or a retreat center or monastery? Instead of going *to* a hermitage, can the hermitage *come* to us?

This is a most reasonable question in that most of us live normal lives of family, work, recreation, and some wider community engagements. And in this, we are more than busy enough. Where, then, does prayer, reflection, and contemplation fit in—if at all?

1. Ringma, *Sabbath Time*.

Preface

I do not in any way mean to minimize the significance of place—such as a monastery, hermitage, retreat center, chapel, or other regular settings for prayer and reflection—but for many of us, these are only *occasional* places. We are usually in these places for an hour or two, a weekend, or a week at the most. And so often, what we experience during a retreat fades when we go back to our normal routines and responsibilities.

So what about our more regular and normal existence? Is that somehow second rate when compared with monks, for example? Is our daily work also an offering to God? Or is prayer more important than our daily activities? And what can a *spirituality of daily life* look like? What are its contours, practices, and challenges? Can one probe the contours of a phenomenology of ordinary spirituality? I believe this is worth doing.

In seeking to answer these and related questions, I am not seeking to spell out a "how to" of daily spiritual practices. This is not about methodology, but reflection. I am seeking to reflect on my own struggles and issues regarding a hermitage of the heart—and I am hoping that by wrestling with these issues, I will give some hope and courage to others.

Life in the daily affairs of human existence is as much a place for prayer and reflection as a monastery or retreat center. And the God of the biblical narratives is as much a God on the road as a God of "special" places.[2]

In thinking about this, I have been struck again by the both/and nature of Christian existence. There is the call to the "cell"—places of prayer—and the call to the "coracle" (a small boat) to enter the world in witness and service.[3] The one relates to the other. Prayer draws us both to God and the world. And the coracle draws us not only into the world, but also to prayer in the midst of service.

---

2. The liberation theologian Jon Sobrino points out that the encounter with God does not only occur in some special space, but "especially in the concrete life of the believer." Ellacuria and Sobrino, eds., *Mysterium Liberationis*, 699.

3. Northumbria Community, *Celtic Daily Prayer*.

Preface

This double movement is clearly reflected in the psalms: "Blessed are those who dwell in your house; they are ever praising you. Blessed are those whose strength is in you, who have set their hearts on pilgrimage" (Ps 84:4–5). Here we see the connection between *being home* and *being on the road*. Or, in other words, being in places of stillness and reflection and also in places of witness and service.

The six-month hermitage time was a special time of being in God's "house." I am now back on the "road." And I am seeking to make better sense of what that is all about. I do so not simply by making my own reflections, but also drawing on some dimensions of the long Christian spiritual tradition, which is such a rich resource for me. Thus the Desert Fathers and Mothers, Celtic spirituality, the Benedictines, St. Francis, and some others will be my companions.

I draw from these companions for several reasons. First, none of us makes the Christian journey on our own. Second, we are born and shaped by the faith community. John Calvin was right, therefore, to call the church the mother of faith. And third, we are far more shaped by various traditions than we realize, and this includes the traditions of Christian spirituality.

I am always deeply indebted to others. My writing companions, the "holy" scribblers—Irene Alexander, Chris Brown, Terry Gatfield, Jill Manton, Tim McCowan, Ross McKenzie, and Sarah Nicholls—deserve unqualified thanks. Karen Hollenbeck-Wuest, who has put her fine editing skills to work, has once again given my writing a more "lilting" tone and a more coherent structure. Pieter Kwant, my ever-positive literary agent, has found a way for this typescript to become a book. And finally, I am happy to dedicate this book to Dianna and Denise, former students of mine at Regent College, Vancouver, whose work sows the seeds for a new tomorrow in the reign of God, which spreads spiritual grounding and healing to all who are its happy recipients.

Brisbane, Australia
2020

Introduction

THIS BOOK OF BRIEF reflections, as I have mentioned in the preface, has been penned in the year or so since my six-month sabbatical, when I spent much of the time in a hermitage.

Over this period, I have been wrestling with the question and practice of what a hermitage of the heart might look like. Put differently, what does a spirituality look like when you are not on sabbatical and can't spend a lot of time in a hermitage? Or, what are the blessings and challenges of a spirituality of daily life?

In reflecting on this, I am not in any way suggesting that I have found the "grand plan" for myself and for my compatriots in the journey of faith. I am merely talking about *my* journey. But if that is in some way helpful to others, I am overjoyed. I do believe that the more honest and reflective I can be about my particular journey, the more my reflections may find resonance with others. After all, the spirituality of St. Francis, as idiosyncratic as that was, has found a universal following.

I am quite sure that nothing in these pages is in any way unique. I am certainly no visionary mystic; seeking to be a follower of Christ is more than enough. Moreover, as followers of Christ, we share a *common journey*, for we have experienced a common "birthing" into the faith, read a common gospel, participated in a common Spirit, and are part of a common faith community. It may also be true that readers from other faiths or those who profess no faith at all may find common themes in these pages. This should not surprise us too much, for we share a common humanity and live on a planet that we all share in common. More basically—and this is a theological statement—we are all made in the image and likeness of God, and therefore we share a common starting point, have a common "being," and are welcomed into a common spiritual identity.

But, of course, there will be differences. In thinking about these differences, I think the best analogy is an orchestra. We are all playing in the same oratorio, but we play different instruments. I am not at all sure whether I am a violin or a flute. I may well be a cello in that I do tend to see the darker side of life.

In my faith journey, I have passed through several naïvetés. What I mean by this is that some of the illusions I used to hold have been shattered. My Sunday school faith had to undergo major changes. My conversion euphoria had to sober up. My optimism about changing the world had to be "bloodied." My Western God had to undergo an Asian makeover. And several extended periods of the "dark night" of the soul have brought me to where I am today—which is a much more fragile faith journey marked by mystery rather than certainty.

The further unpacking of this cryptic statement lies in these pages. I am not so much writing about my ideas or perspectives about the eternal principles of the Christian life, but rather the joys, challenges, struggles, and questions I face as I seek to live a hermitage of the heart, which is about the daily *gestalt* of life. Thus my reflections here attempt to describe a phenomenology of daily spirituality.

May these reflections encourage you at this difficult time in our Western, post-Christendom world. Amidst the increasing marginalization of the church and all the church's internal problems and issues, we are finding ourselves in a *displaced* situation, an *in-between* zone, a *liminal* space. In the words of Northumbrian Celtic spirituality (and the psalmist before them), we are seeking to sing the Lord's song in a strange land.[4]

I happen to believe that this is a good space to be in. In earlier times, particularly in the Middle Ages, the church was a far too

4. Northumbria Community, *Celtic Daily Prayer*.

confident and powerful institution. This is a different era. In this setting, the people of God can be marked by humility, questioning, lamenting, and wrestling with God regarding the way forward.

This is the time to be vulnerable and experimental. I hope that these meager reflections will help us probe deeper so that we might see the renewal of the church, a more just and peaceable society, and greater moves towards the mending of the wounded creation.

However we move forward, the future of Christianity—particularly in the West—will not depend on our institutional prowess, but whether—among other things—we, as laity or clergy, have developed a hermitage of the heart.

But none of us can make the journey of faith, the Christian pilgrimage, on our own. We have a long and fruitful heritage and need companions on the journey. You will meet some of my companions in these pages. May they encourage you as much as they have helped me in the journey of faith.

Our pilgrimage is one of particularity. We must each walk *our own* journey, but there are many guides who can point us in the right direction. May we be open to their wisdom!

1

Embracing the Unexpected

WE ARE COMPLEX CREATURES driven by myriad motivations. Nothing we do is ever simply for "the other," for we also want things for ourselves. It is rather easy to say, "I am doing this for the glory of God," but we all know that much of our love for God is also a love for ourselves. And it is easy to assume that we are doing something without certain expectations, but we know very well that we don't act and do things in a "disinterested" way. We do expect things to come our way.

One of my more or less hidden expectations—hidden initially to myself—was that after my time at the hermitage, I thought my engagement in certain spiritual practices in the midst of ordinary daily life would be easier. This has not been the case. In fact, the opposite has taken place. Everything has become much harder. Setting aside time for prayer and reflection has become a struggle, while at the hermitage it was a most gentle breeze. This has both surprised and upset me.

It is possible, of course, simply to accept this matter and say, "it's just the way it is!" And sometimes, it may be wise to live life this way—just let it be! But we can also seek to make sense of this struggle, which is what I hope to do in these pages. Is there a particular logic at play here? Are there insights we can gain in the contours of our faith journey? Is there a wisdom here that we need to discover?

Unfortunately, embarking on this road is fraught with many questions. To what extent do we simply accept what life brings to us? To what extent should we try to make sense of what happens to us? To what extent do we resist what comes our way? To sharpen this further, to what extent is the faith journey simply one of trust and acceptance? Can we be too reflective? Can this lead to too much speculation? Can this lead to self-preoccupation? These are all relevant questions, which will be explored through these reflections.

What needs to be noted at this point, however, is that my present struggles are not what I expected when I came out of my hermitage time. The *provisional* sense that I make of this is that our relationship with God does not work on a "banking" system. I don't get credit in the bank for having prayed more or served others at a particular time in the past, which then makes the present easier or more blessed. There is no such arrangement.

There are significant reasons for this. The most basic is that my relationship with God is not defined by a commercial transaction, but rather by God's grace and generosity. I am not in a bargaining position with God—where I do something and then expect God to reciprocate in certain ways. Though sometimes I foolishly approach God in this way, not even the Old Testament structure of obedience and blessing can be understood in this way.

The heartbeat of the Old Testament is that I am blessed by God, and my understanding of that goodness moves me to obey God. The movement is not from my good works to God's blessing, but rather from God's surprising and undeserved blessing to an attitude of gratitude from which our actions and service spring.

A further theme at play here is the Lord's prayer for daily bread. What happened at the hermitage is not my bread for *today;* rather, my bread is who I am, what I do, how I receive and give *this* day in my relationship with God and others. Though this perspective is somewhat disconcerting, it invites us into an ongoing newness and freshness in our relationship with God.

This means that I can't live off past achievements—no matter how great and significant they may have been—but only by *present* grace. For example, I can't say, I have prayed intensively for many months, and now I can abandon prayer or assume that prayer will be easier. Nor can I say, I have served the poor for more than twenty years, and now I can live only for myself.

This is all *transactional* language that tries to broker deals with God, and such deals don't work. God is relational. God does not bargain, but provides grace, forgiveness, sustenance, and the presence of the Holy Spirit. This God calls us anew to a living embrace and hope.

The other matter evident in the biblical narratives is that goodness can lead to difficulty and may be followed by trials and temptations. Job's goodness is followed by painful trials. Jesus' baptism ushers him into the desert temptations. The disciples' experience on the Mount of Transfiguration is followed by a failure in ministering to a young boy. The early church's Pentecost experience is followed by persecution. A Christian's sense of the presence of God can lead to the "dark night" of the soul.

Strange as it may seem, this dynamic is a blessing. We can't gain brownie points with God, and we can't rely on the past. We can't create little systems of spiritual predictability. Wheeling and dealing with God is out of the question.

I should have known this. Six months in a hermitage does not magically make the return to "ordinary" life easier. In fact, it may make things more difficult. I am learning this anew.

2

Creative Reappropriation

ARE THERE A NUMBER of ways by which I can seek to build a hermitage of the heart? To put that differently, can I find ways *to repeat* something of the goodness I experienced during my hermitage time?

In seeking to build a hermitage of the heart, I am deliberately using the word *repeat,* but I am not referring to a mechanical repetition. Instead, I am talking about a creative reappropriation.

This distinction is important and can apply to any significant spiritual experience—conversion, baptism in the Spirit, a special calling, a healing, or any other experience of the presence of God through the work of the Spirit.

We so readily try to hold on to what we have received and to live out of its "magic." In other words, we attempt to normalize what was special and to live in a holy bubble. As if that is not enough, we often try to control what we have received and to turn it into a program or methodology.

These impulses bring about many difficulties and can easily sidetrack us, binding us to the past rather than helping us move towards God's final future. They can also make us rely on the special gift rather than the Giver, so that we become more and more demanding, expecting a particular experience of grace to be the normative spiritual reality of our lives. Living in such a bubble can

Creative Reappropriation

blind us to the realities of our world and cause us to judge our brothers and sisters in the faith.

Thus every good gift needs to go through the "needle" of creative reappropriation. What does this mean? God's generous gifts need to be both *received* and *relinquished* so that a particular gift does not become normative for us. We need to lay it down so that we can become open to new possibilities.

But we also need to steward that gift by remaining thankful for having received it, seeking to learn from all that it has given us, and drawing ongoing inspiration from its presence in our lives. This brings the gift into the present in new ways that are not marked by nostalgia for the "good old days."

This is so important. I know some people who are still living nostalgically for a return to the charismatic renewal of the 1960s and 1970s and thus are living frustrated lives in the present.

However difficult, we have to learn how to live God's ever new *present*, to see God's mysterious ways in the here and now.

There are always new ways to reappropriate a particular gift that we may have received in the past as we attend to the present Giver and the future of what may yet be given. There may be new gifts for us to receive and new ways to respond to the changing circumstances of our life and world. This interplay is never static, but always changing.

Wrestling with these issues is a matter of the heart, which opens up new possibilities. Instead of trying to hold onto the Sabbath of the hermitage in my return to normal life, I need to face the new things that may come through a process of creative reappropriation. What did I learn in the hermitage? What can I take with me from there? What can I do in my present circumstances? What do I need to lay down? What new learnings are in front of me? What is the invitation as I return to a workaday world? These are challenging questions, and this book is my attempt to wrestle with them.

But for now, I need to say something more about creative reappropriation, an activity that lies at the heart of the biblical narratives through the celebration of the Jewish Passover and its transformation into the eucharistic celebration of the early church. This feast, which was celebrated by Jesus and his disciples, has become a sacrament of the church, and partaking of it in the worship life of the church has far-ranging significance.

In celebrating the Lord's Supper, I, in faith, receive the living Christ as food and nourishment for the Christian journey. I remember with gratitude his suffering, which has brought new life to me and is life for the whole world. I partake of the bread and wine that point to the future grand supper of the Lamb, where Christ will nourish us in the life of the new heavens and the new earth. Finally, in the common participation of this communion, I acknowledge that I am "bound" to others in a life of worship, service, and care for one another.

This reappropriation of the Eucharist is normative for all other forms of creative reappropriation. My six-month hermitage time also needs to be reappropriated.

In thinking about my hermitage journey, I need to probe its heart and central significance. Was it about prayer? Was it a Sabbath time? Was it about contemplation? What was its heartbeat? Was it about Presence? Was it the desire to be *with*? Was it about rest? These and other questions will need to remain with me.

But the more immediate question is, how can I be with God in a normal day? Can the hermitage be in my heart? Can there be a transfer from that rather "special" time to the more ordinary and mundane?

Tracing this journey in the midst of life will be far more challenging than my months at the hermitage because ordinary life, by its very nature, is less reflective than time spent at a retreat or monastery. But we shall see what unfolds. This is a new adventure!

3

The Jesus Prayer

I AM WONDERING IF the main way to build a hermitage of the heart is through the realm of prayer. After all, that was one of the main activities of my time at the hermitage, where prayer was both a joy and a challenge. Prayer continues to be my biggest challenge now—and maybe it is also the biggest challenge facing the present-day church.

Prayer is challenging because it seems to be useless and ineffective. We pray for many things and situations, and yet so little seems to change. This is particularly true when we pray more specifically, such as, "Lord, please heal my young friend who is dying of cancer"—and then, six months later, we are all at that person's funeral.

Yet I continue to pray, even in the face of its seeming ineffectiveness, and I am seeking to pray more often. Why? My reasons might bring this reflection a little closer to what it means to build a hermitage of the heart.

I pray because I want to and because the gospel calls me to pray. I pray despite its seeming futility and mystery because I *believe* that this is *one* way of relating to God—even the God who seems so distant. I also know that prayer is somehow good for me, but it is more difficult to identify that goodness. Maybe it has to do with placing myself in an appropriate relationship with God, where I acknowledge and seek after God, and I also acknowledge my creatureliness and needs.

Much of my prayer each day is centering prayer, or praying the Jesus Prayer. This is not the Lord's Prayer, but a prayer of the heart using a key word or phrase. For me, at present, I pray, "Lord, have mercy" or "Christ have mercy." Whenever there is a space throughout the day, I pray this prayer, breathing in the word "Lord" or "Christ," and breathing out "have mercy." I am even doing this as I now write. This prayer can become a prayer when I am not praying, so to speak. The Jesus Prayer involves the invocation of the name of Jesus, not in some magical way, but as an expression of a faith relationship.

I can readily segue into this form of praying no matter what I am doing. In praying this way frequently, I slow down and become more reflective. In this way, I become more attentive to God. This way of praying is certainly not grandiose! It is little, a puny offering—and yet it may be more significant than we think.

For now, I am praying the words, "Lord, have mercy. Christ, have mercy." Months from now, I may use another word or phrase. But the present phrase carries a lot of weight or *gravitas* for me.

Most basically, I feel the need to live under the mercy of God. I need God's grace, forgiveness, and healing presence. I need God's support and encouragement. In receiving God's mercy, I enter into the wide spaces of the "smile" of God. Mercy frees me. It is a liberating power. Some may feel that such a cry for mercy goes against our human dignity or minimizes our humanity, and yet this is based on a faulty notion that we are self-sufficient and without error or blame. This is the myth of late modernity, and it is not sustainable at any level of personal reflection or reading of our wider social landscape. There is plenty of madness and injustice in our world—and none of us are without some complicity!

The church in the West may think that we just need better liturgies and programs, but such a pragmatic approach to the Christian life is a myth. What we actually need is to come more fully under the mercy of God. Rather than being a community that happily functions each Sunday as if it has already arrived, we need to become seekers and pray-ers over and over again. We need the presence of God to invade and revitalize us. Whether the church's clergy is ready to encourage seeking and praying instead of promoting programs and strategies remains to be seen, but lay persons are voting with their feet. They are reading books to discover a deeper spirituality, going to spiritual directors to gain insight and guidance, and going on retreats and pilgrimages to renew their faith. Seeking mercy is about being *on the road*, looking for the path of renewal.

Whenever I am praying the Jesus Prayer, I am not only thinking of myself or the church, but I am also holding the whole world in view. And what a world it is! There is much to be thankful for—such goodness and amazing scientific, medical, and economic progress. Yet there is also much to be concerned about, for there are dark specters everywhere: the erosion of the moral fiber in our large and influential institutions, the widening gap between the rich and poor, the polarization and amalgamation of power in the hands of a few elite. There is also the increasingly "dark" side of our technologies, including the loss of privacy in the face of our surveillance societies. And sadly, there is the cry of our "wounded" earth, which we have so exploited.

"Lord, have mercy" is not a prayer for insiders, but a prayer for the whole world—our planet, our societies, our governments, our social institutions, and ourselves.

Within a Christian frame, there is no purely personal spirituality. My life of faith is not simply about God and me, but about a Creator and Redeemer whose concern is for the renewal and redemption of all things.

As I pray this "mantra" of "Lord, have mercy, Christ, have mercy," I do so with deep frustration as well as an underlying hope. Though such a prayer might seem useless, I pray this prayer nonetheless. If God does not even heal my young friend who is dying of cancer, how can I possibly pray for the mercy of God to invade our world so that wars may cease, justice may reign, and peace may prosper? Yet I continue to pray, "Lord, have mercy, Christ, have mercy." Surely this prayer is an expression of a hermitage of the heart.

4

Cultivating Openness

WE CAN GO ON a holiday and be disappointed. We can go on a retreat and be distracted. We can spend time at a hermitage and be bored or frustrated.

This means that while place and setting are important, they are never the whole story. For what we bring to a particular setting in terms of attitude, expectations, and hopes also plays a salient part in our experience.

Thus we need to cultivate a synchronicity between time, place, and our dispositions. We can expect too much—or too little. We can be impatient. We can also have altogether wrong expectations, which happens when we focus on our "agenda" in going on a retreat or spending time in a hermitage or monastery.

We often want a personal "quick fix" of some sort, which reveals that the retreat is about us and has little to do with seeking God and God's purposes. Thus a significant reorientation will need to take place. While God is concerned about us, we are not to be the center of our retreat.

Focusing on ourselves and our interests shrinks and truncates our experience of life. A fuller life is relational. A richer life has transcendent dimensions.

The Christian life is rooted in the grace of God in Christ, and it finds its wider meaning when we intersect our "small" stories with the mega-story of the biblical narratives. In other words, life is fuller when it finds its purpose in the purposes of God for our lives and our world.

Thus it should not surprise us that during a time of retreat, we will need to be decentered and reoriented so that we can find ourselves "anew." That being the case, our disposition will need to be one of openness and receptivity. Put more clearly, we need to be open to being derailed.

Though this is not our favorite pastime—let alone something we seek when we go on retreat—it is part of our journey with God. This is the path of blessing and conversion, though the order is often reversed—conversion first and then blessing. We not only need to be converted from our sins, but also from our "false" self and our illusions. This "undoing" is not a negative strategy, but one that seeks to "reshape" us into a fuller life and a more authentic existence.

That being the case, the pressing question for me is if I can carry that open disposition and receptive attitude into my normal life. The surprising answer is, yes—quite easily. For unlike the occasional nature of a "time out" or a weekend retreat, normal life constantly throws issues, challenges, difficulties, and tragedies at us, and these all invite us into a renewing process. Ordinary life can "undo" us just as easily as a hermitage experience.

Some reorientation might be necessary for us to begin this undoing process. First, we need to overcome the dualistic thinking that divides the sacred from the secular. Transcendence and the presence of God are not limited to a "special" place—the sanctuary, retreat center, or monastery. God is found in the midst of life.

Second, God not only works through "special" events—such as dreams, visions, and miracles—but also through the ordinary events of human existence. Falling in love, the birth of a child, friendship, illness, loss, a particular job, and many other experiences of life can all transform us if we are willing to hear their invitations and bring them into God's presence.

Rather than buffering, safe-proofing, or isolating ourselves in urban ghettoes of privilege, we open ourselves to a richer and fuller life when we "throw" ourselves into the human fray amidst its difficulties and challenges, particularly when we take on the cause of the needy and disadvantaged.

If we invite life itself to "undo" us in this way, our "fuller" self can emerge. This is not happenstance, but the work of the Spirit amidst the beauty and banality of human affairs.

To live this out, we will need to *embrace the ordinary as sacramental*. Thus the ordinary and the Eucharist are both sacred. God is in the midst of both the sanctuary and daily life. My daily life can become a prayer just as much as the time I set aside for prayer.

This means that in every aspect of my life, I need to become open, receptive, listening, discerning. The creation speaks. The Gospels speak. The circumstances of life speak. But they not only speak, they also invite. They say: *come, embrace, receive, learn, grow.*

While the hermitage as a place is valuable, what I bring to it is even more valuable—and the openness, hopes, dreams, and attentive listening that I bring can readily be brought to my daily life as well.

5

The Invitation of the Desert Fathers and Mothers

THE DESERT HAS LONG been part of the Christian imagination. The journey of the Israelites through the desert to the promised land, John the Baptist's desert experience, Jesus' temptation in the desert, and St. Paul's long desert sojourn have all given particular shape to the notion of "desert" in Christian experience.

In the period from 250–400 CE, many Christians began to move into the Egyptian desert to live a life of prayer and asceticism. While first as hermits and later as communitarians, these Christians were the forerunners of monasticism, which had a powerful and formative impact on both the church and Western society.

Initially, these hermits entered the desert in ones and twos, but over time, many followed them. Under the rule of Pachomius alone (c. 290–346), some 7,000 men and women lived in various communities—and there were many other centers as well.[1]

Some of the central impulses of this movement included a desire to follow Jesus, live a life of prayer for the renewal of the church and the world, grow in holiness through a life of surrender and relinquishment, wrestle against the forces of darkness in the world, and become the harbingers of a new world.

1. Waddell, *The Desert Fathers*, 7.

Many in the movement were deeply concerned about the way that the church, which had been marginalized and persecuted in the past, had become a church of the Roman Empire under Constantine. Consequently—and unfortunately—Christianity became a cultural imposition rather than a transformative faith experience.

In our day, there is a growing interest in the Desert Fathers and Mothers, and some present-day "New Monastic" communities look back to this movement as a source of inspiration. They are not suggesting that we go and live in the desert, but that the cultural captivity of the church, particularly in the West, calls us to a deeper life of prayer and spiritual formation as a well as a more countercultural way of life.

I have had a long and growing interest in this movement. Like many other Christians, I was impacted by the charismatic renewal of the late 1960s and early 1970s, which drew many of us into spontaneous times of prayer and fasting that led us to see the injustices of our world more clearly, act more decisively, and make various attempts to live the communal ideal. With this in mind, let us look at some of ways the Desert Mothers and Fathers challenge us.

First, the call to the desert is a call to pray and to embrace a marginal position that dethrones the influence of contemporary cultural values on our lives. This marginality may deepen our dependence on God, help us to engage the biblical narratives more creatively, renew our vision for what our world can become through the purposes of God, and revitalize our mission to the world. Thus the heartbeat of the desert movement does not spring from a desire to escape from the world, but to renew it from a very different operational center.

Second, the movement to the desert recognizes that we can't "fix" the church and society through Christian projects that often reflect the very values that the Christian way is seeking to critique.

Third, the call to the desert challenges the old (and lingering) idea that if the church becomes more socially powerful and significant, it can benefit society more. Rather, the movement

The Invitation of the Desert Fathers and Mothers

places paramount importance on a life of prayer and understands its marginal position as strategic.

Fourth, the movement calls us away from hyper-individualism into a communitarian way of life.

Fifth, this ancient movement teaches us that the Christian way is not about much-having, but about relinquishment and emptiness so that God can fill us anew.

Sixth, the movement helps us to deepen our vision through a contemplative way of life that provokes us to "wrestle" with the spiritual, ideological, and structural powers of our time.

Of course, a lot more could be said about the Desert Fathers and Mothers,[2] but let us hear some of their voices.

Abba John said: "The saints are like a group of trees, each bearing a different fruit, but watered from the same source."[3]

Abba Anthony said: "Our life and our death is with the neighbour. If we gain our brother, we have gained God, but if we scandalize our brother, we have sinned against Christ."[4]

An elder responded to a brother's question, "What is an act of faith?" by pointing out that it is "to live in humble-mindedness and to perform deeds of mercy."[5]

One of the Desert Fathers said: "The Fathers of old went forth into the desert and when [they] themselves were made whole, they became physicians, and returning again they made others whole."[6]

An old desert brother was asked about God's forgiveness. He responded: "Tell me, beloved, if thy cloak was torn, wouldst [thou] throw it away?" He said: "Nay, but I would patch it . . ." The old

---

2. For some reflections on the sayings of the Desert Fathers and Mothers, see Northumbria Community, *Celtic Daily Prayer*, 416–31.
www.orthodoxchurchquotes.com/category/sayings-from-saints-elders-and-fathers/desert-fathers/.
3. https://www.patristics.co/sayings/.
4. https://christdesert.org/prayer/desert-fathers-stories.
5. Quoted in Ringma, *Hear the Ancient Wisdom*, 51.
6. Quoted in Ringma, *Hear the Ancient Wisdom*, 202.

brother responded: "*If thou wouldst spare thy garment, shall not God have mercy on His own image?*"[7]

One of the desert brothers said: "It is dangerous for a man to try teaching before he is trained in the good life."[8]

What we have here is practical Christian wisdom that has been forged through detachment from the world, surrender to God, formation in community, and a life of prayer. Each of these dimensions challenge us today, but the most basic is the counterintuitive call to withdraw in order to pray and reflect so that we can reengage the world and its needs in a more prophetic way.

We Westerners use the opposite strategy. We think that the harder we work, the more we will change society, but our work is so often self-conceived and self-sustained.

The Desert Fathers and Mothers teach us that our service in the world has to be born out of and sustained by the vision and presence of God. I am seeking to hold this vision in my own journey of a hermitage of the heart.

Can you hear the call of the "desert?"

---

7. https://www.goodreads.com/work/quotes/218708-the-desert-fathers-sayings.

8. For further reading, see Merton, *The Wisdom of the Desert,* and Ward, trans., *The Desert Fathers.*

6

Bothering God

I AM VERY AWARE that I ought to be most respectful towards God, the creator and redeemer of the world, who sustains my life and is the One to whom I am fully accountable.

This does not mean that my relationship with God is based on the threat of the Strong One, with me being ever so small in the great scheme of things. Nor am I compelled to respect God from the fear that God will punish me or overwhelm me in some way.

My relationship with God can be wonderfully and surprisingly different when it is based on God's gratuitous love towards me and all that God has made. God is bending towards the entire creation, including me, and giving everything a sustaining and life-giving kiss. This enabling love is expressed in the life-giving Son of God's very heart and the brooding, sustaining, and beautifying Spirit, who is God's inner gift to us.

This means that my respect for God is not for One who is distant, wholly other, or remote. Rather, my respect is for One who has shaped the very fabric of my being and indwells me with a mysterious presence. To some extent, my love and respect for God is a reflection of God's love for me.

Moreover, my respect for God is not meant to strike me dumb, nor to leave me passive or acquiescent before his majesty and glory. Instead, God invites me to be fully myself and to respond to God's greatness with both freedom and commitment. While my love for God is marked by grace, it cannot be a product of coercion.

This creates a wide-open space in my relationship with God, a space that is both reverent and playful, obedient and questioning. This latter dimension is what I have in view when I talk about bothering God.

Abraham bothered God about Lot. Moses bothered God about a vision of God and his troubles with God's people. Job troubled God about his personal and family tragedies and the unhelpful advice from his friends. The psalmists troubled God about his absence. The prophets troubled God about the lack of justice in Israel's communal life. Jesus, who was committed to doing what the Father asked of him, troubled God about his need to suffer.

I am also a God botherer. I do so respectfully—and I do not bother God about my personal circumstances. That looks far too much like complaining. The typical, "God why did you not heal me or provide for me in some special way," is not the miserable dirge that I am singing.

I am singing a different song, one that is also being sung elsewhere, as I sing the Lord's song in a "foreign land." With this song, I acknowledge my pilgrim status. I am an exile here, a sojourner. I have not arrived home, though in faith I have met the great Homemaker.

My song goes something like this.

I am troubled that so many others marked by your creativity have not met you on their pathway. I grieve that our world is so devoid of your beauty, that so much goodness is stillborn, that so much water turns to dust.

I think I should bother you about this—not with answers, but with painful longing. I know of your power, that you can do amazing things. But for the sake of those whom you have created and to whom you given so much freedom of choice, can you be more persuasive?

I know you want us to feel after you, to seek you in humility and faith. I know you call us to abandon our idols. I know you have provided gifts of grace that are ours for the taking.

But you also know how blind we are, how dull of hearing, how self-sufficient, how stupid.

Can you be more persuasive? Don't you intervene? Don't you break up fallow ground? Aren't you the maker of the fertile soil in which the seeds of your kingdom fall? Isn't there such a thing as prevenient grace? Do you need to flatten the mountains and raise valleys to make a smooth pathway? Can't you help us as we stumble aimlessly in all that we have made, amidst all that mesmerizes us?

Can I bother you more? May I, who am made of the dust, provoke you? Or are you displeased with me? Have I overstepped the mark? If so, I am not afraid. Slay me if you must, but revisit your creation with a renewed passion for its urgent recovery in your likeness and beauty. If the human community, with its present self-preoccupation and religious cynicism, won't reach for you, can't you reach out to us?

I don't need to beg you to do this. It is your evident will, for you desire shalom for all and have made provision for all. There can be joy for all. Your banqueting table groans under its bounty. Your invitation has been sent. But please, go out again into the pathways of our lives and persuade us to come and eat. You have great skills in catching us by surprise. You know all too well how to upend us. You can stop us in our tracks. You can appear in power that is forged by a winsome love.

I have no doubts about your ability, but I am concerned about your timing. Don't leave us with our follies for much longer.

It is puzzling, but we need your revelation to grasp what is good for us—and we need your help to get us to sit down at your banquet table.

While these questions have been with me for a long time, they were accentuated during my hermitage time, and they are with me still as I tend the hermitage of my heart. They just won't go away.

7

Becoming

LAST NIGHT I DREAMT about my friend and colleague in the Department of Social Work and Social Policy at the University of Queensland, Dr. Allan Halladay. This man of great goodness asked me to teach a course in business studies—what an irony! I had never taught such a course and was hopelessly unqualified, but I agreed because he asked me. As I struggled to prepare, I felt hopelessly out of my depth. Then I woke up in a cold sweat.

Of course, I should have said "no," knowing I couldn't teach such a course. By saying "yes," I had clearly overextended myself. A similar message has come to me many times and in various ways throughout my life.

During my seminary training days in Geelong, Australia, I agreed to be a part-time high school teacher even though I had not received any teacher training. Later, I began work with troubled street kids and drug-addicted youth with no training in social work. Much later, I agreed to teach at a graduate seminary in Manila to take over a key course, the title of which I did not understand—let alone knew how to teach. I have many more such stories.

Foolhardy? Rash? Presumptuous? Impetuous? *Yes.* Enterprising? Risk-taking? *Maybe?*

But there is something much more important in all this as I struggle with a hermitage of the heart. How does this pattern of behavior fit with the *imitatio Christi* and living the Christian life? What is the relationship between acting boldly and listening to and following the direction of the Spirit? How do we acknowledge the sovereignty of God, on the one hand, and assume human responsibility, on the other? In what ways do we need to come to terms with our human limitations?

While these questions may be theological, there are also existential questions. Does the gift of grace impact or modify our "natural" predispositions? To what extent does personal transformation take place in the life of a Christian?

The fact that I had this dream (and I have had many similar dreams) may suggest that this is still an issue for me, even after all these years. In the words of the Bob Dylan song, "when will we ever learn"?

But rather than being depressed by all this, I am actually encouraged in multiple ways.

First, I am happy that I dream and often remember my dreams. I believe that dreams are a small sign of Immanuel—God with us. I would like God to be more obviously present beyond Scripture, the faith community, and God's strange ways in the world, and so dreams are a gift I am happy to receive.

Second, at the end of the day, I am glad that God does not overwhelm us by making us suddenly "better" and different. When the fiery Saul who persecutes Christians becomes the passionate Paul who brings the good news of Christ to the Roman world, much of who Paul is remains the same, but he is directed in new ways. Moreover, Paul has a profound sense that even more awaits him, for he exclaims, "For while we are in this tent, we groan under our burden, because we wish not to be unclothed but to be further clothed, so that what is mortal may be swallowed up by life" (2 Corinthians 5:4). So I am glad that I am still very much "me," though I need to change more through the grace of Christ.

Third, I am okay with this non-arrival of final goodness in the present life that Paul describes. I think it's a good thing for life to be an ongoing struggle, because it makes life dynamic. There is nothing boring about the persistence of the old, the invasion of the new, and the possibilities of *becoming* somewhat "other" in this strange interplay between the continuation of nature and the creativity of grace. So maybe grace builds on nature after all!

However, I am left wondering what God might think about me overextending myself. Is it just foolhardy? Is it the impulse of life? Is it an act of faith? Is it running ahead of God? Is it bad stewardship? Is it sinful? Does it grieve God's heart?

I don't have any immediate answers, so maybe I am not that impulsive after all!

What is clear is that the hermitage of the heart is not a place of simple security, harmony, and well-being, but a place of turmoil and questioning. The hermitage of the heart is for pilgrims, those who have not settled down in the security of religiosity. I think this is a good thing.

What is equally clear is that the hermitage of the heart is not the product of our own construction. Spirituality within the Christian tradition is not a self-managed project. It is sculpted through intervention, an irruption that may be as gentle as a breeze—or as frightening as an earthquake—as the Spirit of God moves over the waters of the inner chaos of our lives. This Spirit, who works to a self-orchestrated timetable, seeks to bring a new order into our lives.

This means that God's activity in our lives does not obliterate who we are,[1] but redirects, refocuses, and re-creates us, helping us to discover a new center and orientation. Thus we *become* who we were meant to be in the loving but mysterious purposes of God.

May the dreams continue—and may I learn their lessons!

---

1. Maybe this is true of all God seeks to do, which includes a re-creation of a new heavens and a new earth?

8

Calling

THERE ARE MANY DIFFERENT ways to conceive the beginning of the spiritual journey. Some speak of divine encounter, some of conversion, some of coming to faith.

There are also different ways to understand growth and development in the faith journey. Some speak of the path of sanctification, others of growth in holiness. Some conceptualize "ladders" that climb ever nearer to God, and others speak of union with God.

However we may describe the beginning of and growth in the faith journey, it is important to recognize that it has upward, inward, and outward dimensions. The faith journey is never simply about me and my interiority, for it is also about the glory and honor of God. But it is not simply about God either, for it is also about the love of neighbor and the seeking of greater justice and shalom in our world.

Both the beginning and the continuance of the faith journey have their impulse and sustenance in God's gracious action towards us. The genesis of the faith journey is a gift, and it is accompanied by a calling to accept and steward this gift.

While I was brought up in a family that attended church and had certain spiritual practices, particularly reading Scripture and praying at meal times, I still needed to hear, in my later teens, the call to accept Christ and his way of life. Little did I know all that this would mean. But it was a most foundational calling, and it set my life on a particular trajectory, which can be traced as follows.

First, this calling gave my life a transcendent orientation, but more basically, it made me secure in God's love for me. Second, it resulted in my living into the questions, *what does God want with my life?* and *how is God leading me?*

This orientation guided me to look to God for direction in life, which made me attentive to further callings. To spell this out a bit more, I did not think that I had some direct pipeline to God or that hearing God's call would be easy or automatic. Second, hearing God's call often came through a process of reading Scripture, praying, and seeking advice from others. Third, there were times when I thought I was just "bumbling" along and felt only the absent presence of God. Finally, there were times when God's call was more direct.

I will cite two such instances. The first came when I was working in the printing and publishing industry as a compositor in layout and design, and I ended up in the hospital with lead poisoning. During this illness, a very clear thought came to me that I would soon be working with Indigenous communities. Some time later, completely "out of the blue," an invitation came to do this work. I did nothing to make this happen.

Another came years later, when I was in a kind of "no man's" land after theological training, with no clear direction about what to do. In that vacuous space, I one day heard a clear inner voice, "you are on the street, so work on the street." This led me to become a detached street worker in a downtown part of our city of Brisbane, and it eventually led me to set up Teen Challenge in Australia, doing the work of drug use prevention and rehabilitation.[1]

In recounting these two instances—and there were others—I do not wish to suggest that any of this was special. In fact, I wish to suggest that such instances are most ordinary. God calls us—not simply when we are extra good or pious, or in times of retreat or reflection—but right in the midst of our daily activities.

1. See Grant-Thomson, *Jodie's Story.*

This dynamic invites further reflection on the nature of calling. To begin, *why does God call us anyway?* The answer is at least threefold. First, God is a relational God. God relates to him/herself as Father, Son, and Holy Spirit. God is also relational to all of creation and humanity. Second, God loves to make him/herself known through the joy of companionship and delight. Third, God seeks our participation in God's concerns for our world. Simply put, God says, *Come join me in my healing and restorative passion for this world!*

The next question, *what does calling mean for us?*, is rather complex. First, some people might immediately think that they are being told what to do by some heavenly "bully." However, the biblical narratives suggest that God's calling is invitational, because obedience and disobedience are writ large throughout the biblical script. Thus calling not only reveals God's heart, but it also defines us and shapes our life in particular directions for the purposes of the love of God, whose concern is for the healing and redemption of all things.

Finally, calling gives our life its fundamental directional shape. Who I am and what I am meant to do are dynamically interrelated. In fact, what I am meant to do gives shape to who I am. The gestalt of my life—including my inner life—is forged by what I do and how I live. Calling thus unfolds my life. To live with the sense that my life is not simply my own, that I am not simply self-made and self-determined, gives my life a depth of relationality, community, and accountability.

Calling also draws us into a hermitage of the heart. God calls us to pray and to other spiritual practices just as much as we are called to faith and service. This means that in the journey of a hermitage of the heart, a much larger narrative shapes my life.[2] Instead of being and becoming a diminished self, I become an "expanded" self in the calling God.

This will certainly bring challenges. At times, I will want to do my own thing and will resist God's call. At times, I will not want to carry the burden and suffering involved in the call. But by

---

2. See Ricoeur, *Time and Narrative*.

embracing God's often strange ways, I will become more fully who I am meant to be.

The prayer of the Celtic St. Cuthbert is a good companion for this journey.

Lord, I have heard Your voice calling at a distance,
Guide my steps to You, Lord, guide my steps to You.[3]

---

3. Northumbria Community, *Celtic Daily Prayer*, 173.

9

The Invitation of Celtic Spirituality

I HAVE BEEN SIGNIFICANTLY shaped by my family's Reformed heritage and my later theological formation in that tradition,[1] but I have always been attracted to "outliers"—movements at the periphery[2] of the larger Christian story. Why these have attracted me is difficult to understand, but being Friesian rather than mainstream Dutch, and later being a migrant kid in Australia, may have had something to do with it. Perhaps marginality was part of my DNA?

In any case, I later came to believe that groups at the periphery often had something distinctive to teach us. I also came to see that significant change has often been instigated by groups at the margins of mainstream institutions or society as a whole.

Much later, I came to see that marginality is at the very heart of the Christian story. Israel was but a tiny blip on the stage of the ancient world. Jesus was but a Galilean. Christians have been a minority in many societies.

More specifically, Christians are pilgrims who are too late for the world and too soon for heaven. By living in both the now and

---

1. I have always been deeply grateful for my time of theological studies at the Reformed Theological College in Geelong, Australia.

2. I can remember that soon after I came to faith in Christ in my later teens, I was strongly attracted to Count Nicolaus von Zinzendorf and the Moravian movement—and that movement was hardly the main story of Christianity!

the not-yet reality of the reign of God, Christians participate in all the dimensions of life and seek to bless and enhance what is, while at the same time longing and working for a world where swords will be beaten into plowshares.

Given these impulses, it is not surprising that I would be attracted to Celtic Christianity and its small contemporary manifestation, the Northumbria Community in the United Kingdom. Through their liturgical resource, *Celtic Daily Prayer*, and their formation, I have become a companion of this movement in the city of Brisbane, Australia.

I have found Celtic Christianity both attractive and challenging in many ways. I appreciate its foundational Trinitarian theology. I love its emphasis on community and communal spirituality. I find its sense of God in the ordinary so refreshing. The early Celtic Christians prayed prayers relating to every domain of life—lighting the fire, baking bread, milking cows. They saw the great and powerful God stooped amongst them in the common activities of life. For them, creation was the first incarnation, Christ the second, and by way of implication, the faith community is a third incarnation as a sacrament of the reign of God.

The Celtic Christians also held what we today would call a nature mysticism, where creation is God's second hand, and the gospel is the first. Together, these two hands reveal God's beauty and power. In this, the Celtic Christians were panentheistic, in that they understood God to be deeply immersed in the creation as sustainer and renewer, and yet not wholly identified with it. Because of this understanding, their spirituality involved creation care.

Because of their relationship with the natural world, they saw certain places as sacred places. Some of these were regarded as "thin" places, which meant that these places had a sacred presence. This perspective drastically minimized the gap between heaven and earth. Thus the world of the Spirit eked its way into present reality.

Chapels in old monasteries, where monks have worshipped and prayed for hundreds upon hundreds of years, are such "thin" places, but so are places in the created world.

The Invitation of Celtic Spirituality

A few years ago, I had the experience of sitting in a prayer hole on the Island of Lindisfarne, or Holy Isle, in the UK. In these holes, monks used to pray for the evangelization of the Kingdom of Northumbria. I have never felt so "rooted" to one spot and so overcome with the sense of the presence of the Spirit and the Spirit's passion for the renewal of our world.

A further and most important theme in Celtic spirituality was its vision and passion for what we today would call "world evangelization." The Celtic Christians furthered Christianity in what is now the UK and also evangelized much of Europe.

This is a spirituality that a farmer could adopt or a monk could embrace and one that could sustain a missionary embarking on the precarious task of bringing good news to resistant tribal groupings. This is not an inner piety for individuals, but a familial, communal, and missional spirituality.

In the work of social action and the quest for justice, I have been daily sustained by the liturgical resources from the Celtic Christian tradition. Here is a sampling of their wisdom that I have found encouraging.

> *Each thing I have received, from Thee it came,*
> *Each thing for which I hope, from Thy love it will come,*
> *Each thing I enjoy, it is of Thy bounty,*
> *Each thing I ask, comes of Thy disposing.*[3]
> *I am placing my soul and my body*
> *Under Thy guarding this night, O Christ,*
> *O Thou Son of the tears, of the wounds, of the piercings,*
> *May Thy cross this night be shielding me.*[4]
> *Lord, I have heard Your voice calling at a distance.*
> *Guide my steps to You, Lord,*
> *Lord, I have heard Your voice calling at a distance.*
> *Guard my way to You, Lord, guard my way to You.*[5]
> *I arise today:*
> *with the power of God to pilot me,*

---

3. de Waal, ed. *The Celtic Vision*, 31.
4. Newell, *Listening for the Heartbeat of God*, 51.
5. Northumbria Community, *Celtic Daily Prayer*, 173.

> God's strength to sustain me,
> God's wisdom to guide me,
> God's eye to look ahead for me,
> God's ear to hear me,
> God's word to speak for me,
> God's hand to protect me,
> God's way before me,
> God's shield to defend me.[6]

I am deeply grateful for this spiritual tradition, which has deepened my love of God, the Creator, in the beauty of creation. It has challenged me to see ordinary life, including bread baking, gardening, and animal care, as aspects of life held under the smile of God. It has invited me to engage more deeply in spiritual practices, the mystery of friendship and community, and the joy of witness and service.

In the ongoing journey of faith and life, the "Aidan Compline" is an important reminder of the vulnerability of our earthly pilgrimage:

> *I make the cross of Christ*
> *upon my breast,*
> *over the tablet of*
> *my hard heart,*
> *and I beseech the*
> *Living God of the universe—*
> *may the Light of Lights come*
> *to my dark heart from Thy place;*
> *may the Spirit's wisdom come*
> *to my heart's tablet*
> *from my Saviour.*[7]

---

6. Davies, trans., *Celtic Spirituality*, 119.
7. Northumbria Community, *Celtic Daily Prayer*, 31.

10

Hermitage as Place

THOUGH I AM GRAPPLING with what a hermitage of the *heart* might look like, I do think that hermitage as a *place* is important as well.

Yesterday afternoon, I went back to spend several hours at the hermitage on my friend's property. With some good rainfalls over the past months, the bush around the hermitage has become lush, and nature seemed to be wrapping up the hermitage in a blanket of beauty. So I want to talk about place and why it is important.

In the pages of the biblical narrative, we not only learn about places that were important for the Jewish and Christian faiths—the tabernacle, temple, synagogue, and the house communities of the Pauline mission—but we also learn more broadly about creation itself as place for the human community. Earth is our habitat, and it sustains our very life. Who knows, we may well find future habitats in the galaxy.

We are spatial and embodied creatures, and we have both inhabited our world and also built "special" places where faith communities gather, such as churches, cathedrals, monasteries, mosques, shrines, temples, and retreat centers.

So what is the purpose of these special places that we create? What function do they serve? More specifically, what did my friend, Terry Gatfield, have in mind when he built a hermitage on his property?

He told me that he built the hermitage *for* God, to honor God in some way. But there is more to this story. Terry could have built something else to the glory of God. He could have built a monument of some sort. The fact that he built a hermitage suggests that he wanted people to come away from their busy lives for a time of prayer and reflection. He wanted people to seek the face of God in some way. He may well have hoped that people would not only be blessed personally, but that their prayers would be for the renewal of the church and the world.

Possibly, for these and many other reasons, we have created "sacred" spaces not in order to contain God in some way, but to focus ourselves in relation to God. If God is indeed everywhere, then God does not need a temple or a hermitage. But we do! Why is this so? I suggest that while God can be found in the ordinary, we do need to step aside and take time out by going to a "special" place in order to focus on and ground our spiritual practices.

Let me illustrate what I mean. In building a hermitage of the heart, I am seeking to do a number of things at the same time. I am seeking the face of God in the course of my day, but I need to structure these practices as well. Thus certain times of the day need be set aside.

Moreover, while I want to be spontaneous, I am helped by praying, reflecting, and reading in a certain part of the house and a certain spot in the park behind our house. Thus, *place* continues to be important.

What I find interesting about a particular place is that it acts as an invitation. If the hermitage is empty, or the corner of the room where I pray is empty, it speaks to me, saying, *Come! Welcome! It is time!*

But I also believe that "sacred" spaces have a "presence." There have been many places where it has been easy for me to enter into solitude and prayer—chapels in Manila, the Westminster Benedictine Monastery in Canada, the chapel at Schloss Mittersill in Austria, the prayer grottoes on the Island of Lindisfarne in the

Hermitage as Place

UK, the Polish Monastery outside Canungra, Queensland, and many others.[1]

It is interesting to hear that some people are now turning their spare bedrooms into miniature chapels rather than commercial spaces where they can take in another boarder.

As our world, particularly in the West, continues to lunge towards a post-Christendom future and the church continues to be marginalized in society, there is a historical challenge in front of us. The Desert Fathers and Mothers challenge us, because they felt in their hearts the need to inhabit desert landscapes in order to pray for the renewal of the church and for the world. Their sense of urgency was matched by their sense of place—the desert, where all conveniences were stripped away so that they could be with God in great vulnerability.

While going to an actual desert place may not be possible, we can recapture their central motif and embrace their heartbeat. We can embrace the seeming "madness" of these desert pilgrims, who understood that in order to engage the world, they needed to withdraw. To transform the world, they knew they needed to pray. To renew the church, they knew they needed to fast. To gain their lives, they knew they needed to sacrifice.

This depicts a clear vision of the upside-down nature of the kingdom of God, and it is a challenge that is facing all of us, for our Christianity has become too prosaic, too convenient, too similar to the dominant values of secular culture.

Thus our challenge may be to become more out of step and countercultural. This does not mean being different for its own sake, nor for its possible trendiness. I am not suggesting an *extreme* spirituality in the way that we participate in extreme sports or extreme recreational activities.

Rather, I am thinking about a return to the gospel, the way of Jesus, and the example of the saints of the church. I am not talking about the extraordinary. The ordinary is extraordinary enough.

---

1. In these and other places, I have also been able to write. See the preface in *Hear the Ancient Wisdom*.

The call to pray—whether in a "sacred" space or at home, work, or while traveling—is hardly an invitation to hang on a cross. But letting our lives become prayers invites the power of the cross of Christ to work within us. This is what it means to live a *cruciform* life—and surely this is the heartbeat of a hermitage of the heart.

11

Hidden in the Heart of the World

WE ARE LIVING IN the communication age, a time of the greatest externalization of humans in history. Never have so many people been in such regular contact with others, and never have so many people been able—on an hourly or even more frequent basis for some—to put their thoughts, concerns, and pictures into the public arena, where they can be "consumed" globally. As a result, we have become effusive, permanent babblers. Some might say that electronically, "we can talk the hind leg off a donkey."

But this superabundant communication has also caught us by surprise. Rather than feeling deeply connected and appreciated, many people feel lonely. This is partly due to the fact that a deeper human connection is missing. Moreover, we have become overly dependent on receiving responses, feedback, and appreciation from others. In the process of externalization, we have somehow lost—or failed to nurture—our inner selves.

However, we cannot find or nurture ourselves through isolation, but through reflective processes, the gift of transcendence, and discerning relationships.

For the Christian, this means finding oneself in the heart and care of God, the gift of a faith community, and the magnificence of friendship. In this way, we can become deeply grounded. The more we are grounded, the more we can give ourselves to the life and well-being of the world.

Hidden in the heart of God, we are called to be hidden in the heart of the world because the God of the incarnation calls us to love our neighbors and to be like yeast in the world, bringing forth growth and goodness.

Why am I speaking of being "hidden"? The gospel speaks of letting our light shine, bearing witness, and offering service to the world. Surely we need to put ourselves "out there" if we wish to be a healing and reconciling presence in the world.

Of course, this is true, but we also need to tend a hidden life of prayer and acts of goodness that no one knows about. The more we tend such a hidden life, the more we can be truly present for others.

By being in the "heart" of the world, I mean two things. First, I mean being in the midst of life—a banker as well as a baker. A Christian must be willing to enter the whole gamut of economic, political, medical, and other domains of life—not simply in terms of a career, but as a vocation to become the servant of Christ in a particular sphere of life.

Second, being in the "heart" of the world means that we seek to grow in our understanding of the heartbeat of our world. This has to do with seeing the world through the lens of the gospel and in the light of God's healing and restorative justice. It also has to do with seeing the world in both its beauty through the sustenance of God, as well as in its foolishness when it goes its own way. Moreover, it has to do with seeing the world in the light of God's final future.

Beyond the cathedrals and the welfare services of the church, there is a much deeper and greater reality. This is the "hidden" prayer life of Christians and their acts of goodness that are not registered in community newspapers, public broadcasts, and the annual reports of institutions. Most likely, these hidden acts will never appear on Twitter or Instagram. They are the "glue" for a teacher or pupil who seek to pray for and be present to what is happening in the classroom, or someone in the workplace who is trying to encourage a team effort.

No matter how much we struggle with prayer, our prayers—rather than our actions—will beautify the world. To put that more carefully, only our actions that have been birthed and sustained by prayer will bring newness into our tired world.

In the hermitage of the heart, I am struggling with this. Can prayer play such a significant role? Can it really accomplish much? Can it really be beautiful and impactful when it seems so weak and insignificant?

Yet this is the road I am taking. One of the main reasons I am taking this road is that all the other options appear to be much less positive. This does not imply that we should stop our strategies to bring about change in the world. We need to keep going. Yet in all that we have sought to do, so little seems to change.

Contemporary historical examples are telling: the Edsa Revolution in the Philippines, the Arab Spring, the so-called democratization of the former Soviet Union, the multinational companies that have become better global "citizens," the changing culture of banks, attempts to change government policy. The list is endless. There have been so many grand dreams and moves for change, yet the results have been small. Not even churches seem open to significant change!

So as we continue to work for change, against all odds, we also need to reckon with what we *cannot* do. We may change leadership and certain policies, but we can't change the hearts of people. Just think about how difficult it is to change the culture of an organization or movement! Moreover, we can't orchestrate a synchronicity—where many factors come together at the same time—so that change will be significant and lasting.

The dynamics of all of this leads us along the "road less traveled," for it calls us to seek the face of God on behalf of our world. This means we will need to bother God. We will need to assail God with our concerns for our world. This calls us to prayers of *provocation*.

The patriarchs and prophets of old were not passive in their relationship with God. They questioned and argued with God, as did Abraham, Job, and Jeremiah. And throughout the psalms, we hear God being provoked into action.

I need to reflect more on this in the hermitage of the heart. Perhaps provoking God in prayer is like skating on thin ice?

12

The Divided Self

WEEKS AND MONTHS HAVE passed since I embarked on this posthermitage journey to enter a hermitage of the heart more fully. Yet I feel further away than ever from where I would like to be.

My emerging discovery is that I am far more ambivalent and divided than I thought, which is a challenging discovery and rediscovery. I like to think of myself as being committed to seeking to live in God's presence, to being concerned about God's purposes in the world, to prayer and service.

But once again, it is clear that this is a more aspirational than a lived reality. There is a yawning gap between who I want to be and who I am. I seek intimacy with God, but also to do my own thing. I love to read Scripture, but I read it too quickly and flippantly. I desire to pray, but I make myself too busy to do so. My service to the reign of God is often on my own terms. I seem to know so little about seeking the kingdom.

I find all sorts of excuses. I blame God: *why don't you work more powerfully in my life?* I blame the church: *why aren't you a more dynamic institution?* I blame my Christian friends: *why don't you challenge me more?*

But none of this gets me anywhere, for this is not someone else's problem. It is mine alone. Thankfully, I can acknowledge this in God's presence and join Paul in his brutal confession: "Wretched man that I am! Who will rescue me from this body of death"? (Rom 7:24). It remains to be seen if I can also share his confidence: "Thanks be to God through Jesus Christ our Lord!" (7:25). I don't feel rescued at all. In the midst of this ongoing struggle, a hermitage of the heart seems like an impossible dream.

In grappling with this struggle as I seek to probe a phenomenology of daily spirituality, I wonder if there is an underlying problem with the expectation of *progress* in the Christian life. Yet the New Testament clearly implies that we are called to *grow* in maturity in Christ, and progress is a central theme in the long history of Christian spirituality. There are models of climbing a ladder to greater sanctity. There are themes of growing from a love of God for ourselves to a love for God for God's sake. There is the theological shift from justification to sanctification. And there is John Bunyan's *Pilgrim's Progress*.

Becoming more Christlike is clearly part of our calling, but we may need to reflect more carefully about how we understand this and what this call to maturity looks like.

Maybe I misunderstand "maturity." Maturity may mean that I exhibit a greater childlikeness of faith, or that I feel more vulnerable and less able, that my life is more of a struggle. With the Anabaptists, it could mean that I live with less victory and certainty and more with *Gelassenheit* (yieldedness) to the strange ways of God with us, including mystery and suffering.

Thinking about all this helps me somewhat, but I am still a "divided" self. I both long for intimacy with God, and I want to go my own way. I love the gospel, and I question it. I want to serve God's purposes in the world, and I also want to make life easy for myself. This is what I do! This is who I am! If I don't acknowledge these things, I am seriously missing the boat.

More fundamentally, this struggle seems to be part of the faith journey. We live an ongoing dialectic between attraction and resistance, longing and stubbornness, renewal and conformity.

Maybe this tension is good rather than bad. There are myriad dangers for those who think that they have reached perfection and have a special "hotline" to God. Human pride is already embedded in the human condition, and if we make assumptions about our divination, it will become even worse. As the pages of history confirm, having both social and godlike power is a volatile cocktail. We only need to think of the apocalyptic religious figures who have led people astray—such as Jim Jones and the mass murder of his followers in Jonestown, Guyana—or political figures who assumed religious stature—such as the Roman emperors at the time of Jesus or Stalin and Hitler in the twentieth century.

Rather than making godlike claims, Christian maturity confesses our ongoing reality as sinner/saints, to use the language of Martin Luther. It is far more insightful to recognize our "pilgrim" status. And it is truer to the gospel to see that fullness of life lies in God's final future.

But none of this makes me feel any better now—nor is it a cop-out. I can't say, *Never mind the mess I'm in now. I'll just wait for God to make it all right in the great beyond.*

So I feel sad and troubled. I want to live more fully in God's way, but I fail. And so I try to become more open and prayerful to what God may yet do in my life. I cry about my "divided" self and my lack of Christ-conformity. I need God's forgiving grace and empowering Spirit.

Living a hermitage of the heart is not an easy journey, but the journey continues!

13

Engaging the Ordinary

So much of the daily rhythms and duties of life are ordinary. So much of our life is about maintenance rather than scintillating creativity.

When something creative does take place, it quickly becomes structured, both in the life of the church and the broader society. The fragile Pauline house churches of early Christianity soon became the basilicas of the ancient world. Later revival movements became denominations. Nascent spiritualities soon became a structured way of life for the followers who were formed in that way of life. In the broader society, new social ideas become political parties. Self-help groups become major service providers. Family businesses morph into corporations. After the revolutionaries come the bureaucrats!

As we live our personal disciplines and familial routines within these structures, it gives our social life a sense of permanence and predictability. In and of itself, this sense of structured ordinariness is wonderfully good, and we should accept it with gratitude. In fact, the Benedictine way of life is all about the spirituality of the ordinary, focusing on Jesus during the Nazareth years rather than his public ministry, or the life of Joseph rather than Mary. Throughout Christianity, many unknown Desert Fathers and Mothers, monks, and "ordinary" Christians up to this day have lived a life of faith in quiet and unassuming ways—and they are remembered no more, except in the heart of God.

Yet we have a problem with the ordinary and forgotten in our modern world. We want to be known, acknowledged, significant, and remembered. We want to leave historical "traces" through our art, writing, or other ways of self-preservation.

I wish I could say that this isn't true for me, but that would be less than honest. I, too, want to be remembered beyond my immediate family.

So is our need to be acknowledged and remembered all about our social personas and fragile egos? Are we just trying to "cheat" death? Do we need to feel valued? The answer to these and related questions is simple enough: yes!

This leads to my next inevitable question: is this need for significance healthy in the development of a hermitage of the heart? The immediate pious answer is, "no." Yet I disagree. Though the hermitage of the heart should not be all about my ego, the need to be significant and remembered is fundamentally human.

If we read the early chapters of the Genesis narrative symbolically, we may conclude that the human condition, which is birthed in love and in relationship with the Creator God, becomes soiled, and this results in our alienation from God. Expelled "from the garden," we long for home. Though we hide from God, we long to be found. Marked by mortality, we long for eternity. Unknown wanderers, we long to be known. Our desire for significance is a dominant theme in this symbolical tapestry.

Poor us! This is all quite pathetic!

In the hermitage of the heart, we wrestle with our desire to be known and its many related themes: the nature of spiritual homecoming, the call to repentance, the dynamics of inner healing, our growth in Christlikeness, our life in the Spirit, the challenge of spiritual practices, and how we can act in our world as peacemakers on the journey towards justice, shalom, and the flourishing of all creation. By engaging these matters, we find our true significance.

Thus our longing for significance is only a problem if we are only concerned with self-creation and self-orientation, always begging others, *please notice how important I am!* Our longing for significance is not a problem when it is other-directed.

This means that my significance does not reside in myself, but in the grace and love of God and in the beauty that I am known by the One who brings me home. My significance is found in the wonder of who I am in my relationship with Christ as I discover who I am in the purposes of God for our world.

Clearly this is a very different kind of significance, where I find my purpose in the grace, call, and empowerment of the Great Other, the God who in Christ became one of us, that we might belong to him.

This is easier said than lived! Though the grace of God in Christ shapes and orients us, we are always mere beginners in the journey of faith. We continue to be self-seeking. And as "sinner/saints," to use the language of Martin Luther, we continue to be divided selves.

But the hermitage of the heart is a place where we agree to face our self-seeking, divided selves honestly. Dealing with this reality means that the hermitage of the heart is not a static place, where we celebrate our so-called spiritual progress, but rather a place of ongoing turmoil and conversion.

Rather than seeking a self-congratulatory spirituality that gives us a false sense of significance, in the hermitage of the heart, we drink continually at the fountain of grace, where we find our purpose and are empowered to live out of that inspiration anew.

14

The Invitation of Benedictine Spirituality

ST. BENEDICT OF NURSIA (c. 480–550), the "godfather" of the Benedictines, founded the monastery of Monte Cassino in 529. Other Benedictine monasteries then began to multiply throughout the known world at that time. These communities provided both religious and social stability amidst the collapse of the Roman Empire.

Benedictine monasteries are still with us today. One of my favorite Benedictine communities is Westminster Abbey near Mission, British Columbia. My retreats at this monastery not only impacted me, but also the students who signed up for courses in Christian spirituality.

I want to focus here on several lessons I learned from the Benedictines and how those have impacted my ongoing journey of a hermitage of the heart.

The Blessedness of the Ordinary

One abiding theme in Benedictine spirituality is to live the ordinary extraordinarily well. While this may sound counterintuitive, because we might expect the things of the Spirit—and hence much of the Christian life—to be amazing and different, the reality is that much of the Christian life is about family, relationships, work, and our involvement in daily affairs.

Thus we need to have a sense that our ordinary selves are well-loved by God and that the daily activities of our lives are pleasing to God and under God's beneficence. In this light, we can see preparing a meal as a "priestly" task that we not only offer to our family and guests, but also to God.

Seeking the presence of God in daily life—not only in a special place or activity—is an important theme for a hermitage of the heart.

Monastic Mindfulness

As we learn that God's presence and surprises are embedded in our most ordinary days and common activities, we begin to grow in *attentiveness*. In this most challenging practice, we seek to become aware of what God is doing in the present—the here and now.

In order to cultivate this practice, we need to become not only less rushed and compulsive, but also more reflective and recollected. A reflective and recollected posture will lead us into stillness and a silence of the heart, where we can hear and see what we might fail to notice otherwise.

Growing in attentiveness is one of my biggest challenges. Moving forward and doing more is my way of operating in the world. Stepping back and reflecting is much more difficult.

Life's Rhythms

In our modern world, we tend to live distracted lives that may be out of balance. We tend to overdo one thing at the cost of another.

We can learn much about focus and balance from the Benedictines, who live a rhythm of *prayer*, *study*, and *work*. They integrate the practice of solitude with the gift of community. They are concerned about the gift of the earth in their farming practices, and their vision is for God's final future in the world to come.

The Benedictine commitment to *prayer* is outworked in liturgical prayer as a gathered community, private prayer, and prayer in the midst of their work of farming, educating, hospitality, and spiritual direction. Clearly both private prayer and prayer in the midst of daily life are important for a hermitage of the heart. For in the hermitage of the heart, prayer is not simply about asking God to deal with matters that concern us, but, first and foremost, a form of communion that acknowledges the God who is with us. Such a spirituality of prayer is central to being a Christian.

A commitment to *study* expresses our love for God with our minds as we read Scripture, reflect on it, and seek to think the thoughts God has for the world. In other words, as we make time to read and reflect on the rich biblical and theological heritage of the church, our study will guide us about how to be and act in the world. Such a spirituality of study forms our minds in godly wisdom and gives us a vision for action wherever we find ourselves in the world.

A spirituality of *work* is intrinsic to the Benedictine tradition as well as other monastic traditions. Throughout history, monasteries have developed agriculture, run guest houses for pilgrims, cared for the sick and infirm, run schools and trained clergy, copied manuscripts, and encouraged art and music. Their work has shaped the world, and through it they have seen themselves as co-creators with God. Thus our work does not define who we are, but expresses our love of God and neighbor.

This spirituality of work is connected with a spirituality of *rest*, Sabbath, or holy leisure. This rest is not a time of recuperation so that we can do more work, but rather a form of worship and openness to God. This spirituality of rest also helps shape our hermitage of the heart, for as we rest from our own work, we enter into the beneficence and care of God.

Benedictine Wisdom

Following is some wisdom that has encouraged me in my journey of a hermitage of the heart.

A Fragile Hope

Place your hope in God alone. If you notice something good in yourself, give credit to God.[1]

Great care and concern are to be shown in receiving poor people and pilgrims, because in them more particularly Christ is received.[2]

The Rule knows much about the continuing paradox that all of us need to be both in the marketplace and yet in the desert; that if we join in common worship yet have also to be able to pray alone; that if commitment to stability is vital so also is openness to change.[3]

We are essentially rhythmic creatures, and life needs this rhythm and balance if it is to be consistently good and not drain from us the precious possibility of being . . . our whole selves.[4]

The Benedictine concept of humility, which is based on an "awareness of the presence of God" at work within us, is an "antidote to an achievement-driven" and "image-ridden competitive society."[5] Thus Benedictine spirituality encourages a hermitage of the heart, for it teaches us that "life is not a regimen to be endured. It is an enterprise meant to be made possible, made beautiful at every stage." This includes the invitation to "co-creation, the human commitment to continue the work of God on earth," including "to tend the land and conserve the waters . . . [to] enhance all life now and preserve them for later generations."[6]

The Benedictine tradition is an enduring Christian spirituality that is an antidote to religious extremism, individualism, and a life out of balance. It sees God in all things, knows the disciplines of prayer, sees ordinary work as sacramental, is committed to earth care, and encourages us to a rhythmic way of life that calls us to long-term perseverance.

---

1. Fry, ed., *The Rule of Saint Benedict*, 13.
2. Fry, ed., *The Rule of Saint Benedict*, 51–52
3. de Waal, *Seeking God*, 29.
4. de Waal, *Seeking God*, 93.
5. Chittister, *The Monastery of the Heart*, 171, 170.
6. Chittister, *The Monastery of the Heart*, 124, 116.

15

The "Normal" Christian Life?

I HAVE BEEN WONDERING whether the language of a "hermitage of the heart" is a little too fanciful. Maybe what I am exploring is simply how to live the Christian life amidst the more normal realities of life.

This may well be the case, but I think we need to be careful with this kind of language. What is normal for one person is not normal for another. To live in a monastery is normal for a monk, who must also face questions about how to live the Christian life within the rhythms of a monastic community. Yet many of us would see such an existence as anything but normal!

By way of extension, a Christian who is in prison for having committed a crime, a Christian peasant farmer in Asia, and a Christian prime minister in the UK all live in very different circumstances. Yet these examples are hardly normal, either. Though all are called to live the Christian life in the realities of their daily circumstances, the farmer would face very different challenges than the prisoner or the prime minister.

So the language of how to live the Christian life amidst the "normal" realities of life may not be all that helpful. The issue that concerns us is how to live the Christian life amidst our particular life circumstances, life stages, and the changes that will inevitably come our way. This means that we will need to make adjustments, face new challenges, and learn new things. And we will need to do all this in relationship with others, for the idea of the solo Christian flies in the face of God's vision to build a *people* who will reflect something of God's glory in the world.

Within this frame, we should ask if there is such a thing as a "normal" Christian life. This question invites a whole range of responses.

First, there is nothing normal about the Christian life. It is hardly normal to acknowledge that there is a God, or that we need to be saved, or that God's salvation comes through Jesus dying on the cross as a common criminal. It is also not normal to devote our life to serving God. Nor is it normal to forgive others, sacrifice, or live to bless other people. It is actually quite unusual to live this way.

Second, if by "normal" we mean "common," we are faced with a further question: do we all share a common Christian life? Or, much more pointedly, is there a form and shape of the Christian life that is common to all of us? This calls for both a qualified "yes" and "no." Yes, all Christians share a common faith in Christ, a common call to become more Christlike, and a common call to serve others for the sake of the kingdom of God. But there are also many differences amongst Christians. For example, some are pacifists, some are communitarians, and the rest of us (oddly enough) might regard ourselves as more "normal" Christians.

In coming back to my initial question, it may be more accurate to say that probing a hermitage of the heart is how I am seeking to live the Christian life in the present circumstances of *my* life. So what does that look like?

Right at the outset, I need to say that it looks pretty normal. I have a family. I work part-time. I have friends. I grow vegetables. I go on holidays. I have a roof over my head. I go to church. Being a Christian doesn't really herald an immediate standout unless one wears a Franciscan habit or dresses like the Amish.

It is also not very unusual that I have been on a bit of a spiritual quest. Life in our contemporary world has become more and more functional and pragmatic, which has sucked the beauty and inspiration out of our lives. As a result, many people have begun to seek some form of a sustaining spirituality. My quest has led me down a particular road in that I am particularly interested in both Franciscan and Celtic spiritualities.

My interest in certain issues is also pretty mainstream. My concern for the environment means that I am seeking to live a more careful lifestyle, travel less, and plant rainforest trees. My concern for justice means that I am involved in refugee issues. I also maintain a commitment to teach in Asia so that I can learn from the faith communities there.

Though I could go on, much of what I do and who I am is similar to many other people, including those of other faiths and those who claim to have no religious convictions at all.

But there is a *particularity* to how I am seeking to live. I have had a faith encounter with Christ, and so I live out of the Christian tradition and believe that the Spirit will sustain and guide me. I read the biblical narratives because I believe that they contain wisdom, and I am seeking to live out of that wisdom. However, I do not accept a flat reading of Scripture, meaning that all of its sayings have equal value. Many of the earlier Old Testament precepts and ceremonies are no longer relevant for us. I read Scripture backwards from the Christ event and forwards to God's eschatological future.

I believe that Christ is not only my Savior, but also the normative human being, whose life inspires me to live in certain ways, and so I struggle with what it means to become more Christlike. But the truth is, when it comes to living in the way of Christ, I feel as if I am in kindergarten.

I also believe that Christians should participate in all the dimensions of life—including the economic, political, and artistic—not only to serve our families and the wider community, but also to be signs, servants, and sacraments of the reign of God. From this perspective, we participate in all of life so that we can bring something of the love and goodness of God into the world.

Furthermore, I feel strongly about the importance of living a *prophetic spirituality*. We cannot just accept the way everything is in our world. Though there is much goodness and beauty, there is also distortion and madness within our social fabric. Thus Christians need to be a "disturbing" presence in the world, called not only to announce good news, but also to denounce what is unjust. Most importantly, we need to live the change we wish to see.

My biggest challenge has been—and will continue to be—to live as fully as possible in the way of Christ and to do what God calls me to do. *Lord, have mercy. Christ, have mercy.* What is "normal" about any of this?

16

Discouragement

THERE IS NOTHING TRANQUIL about this day, though I have regular routines that are meant to "steady the ship," so to speak. But some days are just different, and this has a lot to do with how I *feel*—though various psychological tests suggest that I am more of a thinking, rather than a feeling, person. But I often feel deeply, especially about justice issues.

And today, I feel deeply discouraged. I am struggling with this feeling, since nothing untoward has happened. The sky has not fallen in, and there are no changes in my outward circumstances.

In fact, I should be joyful and thankful, for I am well cared for in every way and have the health and energy to be engaged in a range of activities, including my happy pastime of writing.

It is never easy to "drill down" and discover what is really going on inside ourselves. We are all complex, have many defense mechanisms, and are often blind in relation to ourselves.

But I wonder whether discouragement is both generic to the human condition and particularly true of Christians. Let me explain.

The human condition is a strange mixture of ease and frustration, hope and disillusionment, satisfaction and discouragement. We are both grateful and dissatisfied. I believe that this is because we are marked by eternity, but we have fallen out of God's hands. No matter what we have received, we long for more, and we constantly project what could be into the future. We can easily become discouraged when all that we long and hope for does not come our way.

In many ways, I think that Christians are even more susceptible to discouragement because we have tasted something of the grace of God, the life-giving power of the Spirit, and the goodness of the age to come. Thus we are living in an *intermediate* zone—towards this age to come, but not fully there; home in God, but not yet at our final destination; on the way, but still pilgrims. We often live with the sense that we have hardly progressed at all.

Thus discouragement seems to be generic to the Christian experience. We can't just hope, because we also experience reality. This constant delay of our hope in the fullness of life, the return of Christ, the fuller coming of the kingdom of the God, and the greater manifestation of the life of God in our churches and world can lead us to frustration and discouragement. Maybe this delay *should* lead us to discouragement, because otherwise, we will have fallen asleep and accepted the way things are.

Yet I wonder if there is more to my discouragement. Have I taken the easy road? Have I done enough? Have I been faithful to God's call? Have I loved enough? What about my life of prayer and sacrifice? Have I followed the strange nudges of the Spirit? These kinds of questions can easily lead me to discouraging answers.

Of course, these questions are followed by counter themes. Obviously, the Christian life does not depend on me, and the goodness of God is not based on my righteousness. God works despite me, and grace is abundant.

As I wrestle with these things, I know that I will not spiral toward solutions. So today, I let myself feel a sadness about my life and the human condition. I let myself feel discouraged about the state of world—so confident in its self-justification and abilities, yet so marred and flawed.

And I bring my feelings of discouragement to God. The hermitage of the heart is not only a place of bright colors and joyful melodies, but also a place of shadows and songs of lament. What could be is not yet. What I long for is still in the dim distance. The journey of faith has merely begun. The "promised" land is but a specter. My personal well-being still carries scars—and sometimes open wounds. Social goodness and the common good are still marked by injustice.

Despite my discouragement and struggles, I know that my discouragement is not a bad thing. Though it can spiral out of control, it is a reality check, a necessary counterbalance to blind self-satisfaction, and a fundamental nature of the human condition. Surely it is better to be discouraged than indifferent, in denial, or full of illusions.

Maybe what matters is not what "state" we are in—happy or discouraged, at peace or in turmoil, full of faith or struggling with doubt, in the light of God's presence or the dark night of the soul. Rather, what matters is where this "state" takes us, how we respond to it, and to whom we take it.

Long ago, I came to the conclusion that God can cope with my "stuff"—including my wrongdoing, questions, and doubts. God is not a fragile, sensitive "personality" with whom we need to be culturally correct at all times.

Perhaps we need to become more up-front about our faith journeys, struggles, and issues. Maybe we are suffocating from all our middle-class, anemic, and prosaic piety.

My experience of the prayers and sentiments of the poor in the majority world provides a very different picture. They don't have our "pious" language and can be brutally honest with God. They are up front about their needs and express their disappointments when they feel that God has let them down.

From them, I have not only learned to speak to God much more directly, but also to become more honest with myself. Maybe our self-sufficient and bland piety has pushed God to the periphery of our lives? Maybe we need to find more honest ways to talk to God?

Today, I am discouraged. Tomorrow will be a new day.

17

Living an Ascetic Spirituality

THE HERMITAGE OF THE heart, or my spiritual interiority, is not a blissful and unruffled place. I don't think it is possible—or even desirable—for us to reach some permanent, glasslike sea of an internal haven. For as we move towards greater authenticity and maturity, there will be ongoing internal turmoil, and we will always be buffeted by whatever is happening around us because we are called be involved in the issues of our time.

The questions that I ask as I seek to live the Christian life amidst such times of turmoil are, *what do I need to receive,* and *what do I need to sacrifice?* For surely the Christian life is not only about receiving the grace and mercy of God!

This challenge gives Christian spirituality a particular flavor, for it is not simply about self-enhancement, but personal transformation through the healing presence of Christ. As we become "new," we seek to imitate Christ by doing the will of God in our time.

As we seek to imitate Christ, we will inevitably need to make changes and sacrifices, and such considerations usher us into the domain of asceticism.

Initially, we may be tempted to give asceticism a very wide berth, but it is part of the Christian tradition, and its purpose is to help us become more Christlike through rigorous training and self-discipline. For an athlete, such training involves making sacrifices, for you will never become a good athlete if you eat junk food and spend too much time in bed!

So what does this mean for me? First, I need to focus on some generalities. Because I am rooted in the broader church and faith community, I can simply accept and embrace certain things from the tradition rather than trying to invent them. For example, there are several basic spiritual practices that frame asceticism, including observing the Sabbath, giving, praying, fasting, being available, and extending hospitality.

At a more personal level, certain ascetic practices may be more prevalent during an earlier phase of life, while other practices may dominate a later phase of life. When we were young, my wife and I, together with our family and friends, spent several decades providing hospitality for street people with drug addiction issues. Later, we spent more time in the formation and training of others. In our current phase of life, we have become more reflective and prayerful.

This raises another matter, which is that we do not tend to hold various practices together well. We often get things out of sync. When hospitality is not complemented by appropriate withdrawal, self-care, and prayer, we can do damage to ourselves and others. And it is hardly healthy to spend all our time praying while closing our hearts to a needy world.

So what are the pressing issues and challenges to living an ascetic spirituality? First, we need to remember that asceticism is not God's demand, but an invitation, a "free play." Second, we need to remember that asceticism has nothing to do with righteousness. We can't earn credit in God's bank, for all is grace.

At its core, ascetic spirituality is very simple. First, I voluntarily lay aside a certain "good" in order to create space for something else. To give one example, I stop the good work that I am doing in order to spend time with another person for that person's sake. Or I make time to pray when I could be doing other "important" things.

Second, I do things that I do not speak about. The gospel instructs us to do kind deeds in secret, not to let our left hand know what our right hand is doing.

Third, I constantly need to challenge my internal justifications. One justification for me is that because I am a pensioner, I don't have much in terms of financial resources, and so I can't give much to others. We can always argue that we have less than others, but this justifies a closed heart and closed hand. To be generous when we have much is one thing, but to be generous when we have little is something else altogether. I have learned this goodness from being with the poor, who have shown me generosity out of their poverty!

There are many challenges with how we view money and possessions, how we listen and respond to nudges of the Spirit, and how we view others in need. We need to discuss and reflect on these issues more within the faith community so that we can express them more fully in our spiritual practices.

There are also some wonderful surprises. For rather than diminishing us, ascetic practices actually enhance us. When we give money, time, or attention away, we do not stultify ourselves, but become more humane, more Christlike, and more committed to the common good. There is also overwhelming evidence that ascetic practices are good for our health and general well-being. What good news!

Because I was brought up with a strong Protestant work ethic, I need to hear the ascetic challenge of a Sabbath spirituality. I have come to learn that embracing this rhythm is good for my well-being—as is fasting from time to time. We have also received great "riches" of conversation and sharing through the practice of hospitality.

These discoveries suggest that when we embrace certain ascetic practices as a discipline (rather than a punishment), they can ground and orient our lives. And when we embrace them freely, they can provide space for the unexpected to emerge. For living an ascetic spirituality breaks the tyranny of immediateness, productivity, and achievement, myths that dominate our contemporary lives.

Asceticism is profoundly countercultural, but it may well sow the seeds of a better tomorrow. In the meantime, a hermitage of the heart demonstrates sacrificial practices that are hidden from the calculating mind.

18

The Invitation of the Anabaptists

THE ANABAPTISTS HAVE INTRIGUED and challenged me throughout my life. In the beginning of my third year of theological studies, I suddenly wondered why—if the Anabaptists were such a deviant Christian group—my Reformed professors kept bashing them rather than simply ignoring them?

This thought led me to begin reading the Anabaptists for myself, often in the dead of night, when my other academic work was done. What I read impressed me: their dedication to listen to the Gospels, their formation of communities, their stance against violence. I soon came to see why they were perceived as "enemies" by the emerging mainstream Protestant traditions and the state. Yet their willingness to suffer was an inspiration to me, along with their courage in challenging the politics of their day.

In the subsequent years, as I worked alongside others with street people, troubled youth, and those with addiction issues, the Anabaptist tradition inspired us in two ways. First, it inspired us to create communities of care for those who were seeking to deal with their addictions, sharing a common life with them as much as possible, thus rejecting an institutional model of service provision. Second, it inspired us to deal with justice issues by confronting corrupt government agencies. This stance caused us to suffer. Most

Christians understand the healing ministry; they don't always understand the work of justice.

Thus far in the story, I had not met an Anabaptist or Mennonite. That happened several decades later, while I was teaching at Regent College in Vancouver, Canada, where I had many Mennonite students who saw themselves as evangelicals and did not know the richness of their own tradition. I also met John Toews, who was a professor at Regent. He and his wife, Lillian, were amazing in their practice of hospitality and also in their example of non-retaliation, as they had to sell their house at a greatly reduced value due to First Nations claimants. I was impressed with the way they lived the Anabaptist dictum of *Gelassenheit* (yieldedness) to the strange purposes of God in daily life.

Many themes stand out for me in the Anabaptist tradition. First, God's gift of grace in Christ does not lead to a life of privilege, but a life of discipleship. Second, we are called to follow the lowly Christ, rather than the triumphant Christ, into the world. Third, God is a community-forming God, and so community is part of living the Christian life. Fourth, I cannot live the Christian life without also keeping the needs of my brothers and sisters in the faith in view. Fifth, in living the Sermon on the Mount, I call in question the dominant ethics of our time. Sixth, peacemaking, rather than warmongering, is to be the basic ethic of the Christian. Of course, a lot more could be said, but here I will reflect on this spiritual tradition in relation to a hermitage of the heart.

With its emphasis on the lowly Christ, this spiritual tradition encourages the hermitage of the heart as a lowly place. It is not a place to develop our egos, concoct grand plans, or harness power.

With its focus on Christ as the Prince of Peace, this spiritual tradition promotes a vision of the hermitage of the heart as a place to lay down our rationalizations, aggression, and retaliation issues.

With its emphasis on following in the footsteps of Christ as the one who heals and reconciles, this spiritual tradition seeks to build relationships and community. Thus a hermitage of the heart moves us beyond individualism towards hospitality. Even in our alone time, we bring others with us into the presence of Christ, the Good Shepherd.

A hermitage of the heart that is formed by this tradition does not seek to control things and others, but lives with open hands and a *Gelassenheit* (yieldedness) to God, into whose hands we place our lives in simple trust.

Finally, a hermitage of the heart that is shaped by this tradition not only cultivates a soft heart towards God and others, but also a steely heart that resists the powers of our age.

Following is some wisdom from Anabaptist voices:

Anabaptist testimonials are examples of existential Christianity, meaning the unity of faith and life, and the very absence of despair and anxiety even in the face of death.[1]

It is this martyr-mindedness which gave Anabaptism its particular quality and character.[2]

While mainline Reformers rediscovered the great Pauline term Glaube (faith), the Radical Reformers rediscovered the evangelist's word Nachfolge (discipleship).[3]

It was this biblical grounding—this thorough owning of the biblical text and story—that was the source and foundation of Anabaptist spirituality.[4]

Whoever wants to rule with God must be ruled by God. Whoever wants to do God's will must set aside his own. Whoever wants to find something in God must lose as much in himself.[5]

It is little wonder that the Anabaptists were called the "Radical Reformers" of the Reformation. Several key understandings set them apart in the world of that time, when the Christendom model of church and society was alive and well. First, they understood that they were following the suffering Christ into the world. Second, they understood that baptism included the baptism of blood (martyrdom). Third, they understood that following Jesus

1. Friedmann, *The Theology of Anabaptism*, 31.
2. Friedmann, *The Theology of Anabaptism*, 56.
3. Shenk, ed., *Anabaptism and Mission*, 53.
4. Snyder, *Following in the Footsteps of Christ*, 122.
5. Hut, quoted in Snyder, *Following in the Footsteps of Christ*, 41.

required a commitment to peacemaking, shared community, and a sharing economy.

In the hermitage of the heart, this tradition reminds us that the radicalness and suffering of Jesus does not allow us to escape from the world, but plunges us into both its beauty and its madness.

19

A Sabbath Spirituality

NOTHING SUBSTANTIAL IS EVER done or built swiftly, be it a building, community, or the spiritual practices that form a hermitage of the heart.

Good things come slowly, and they often have to pass through the needle of difficulty and discouragement. This means that we have to find a way to keep going even when we may want to give up.

One thing that has kept me going in my hermitage of the heart has been to establish Sabbath spaces in my daily routine—or sometimes my lack of routine. I'll first say a few things about Sabbath spirituality before talking about my challenges in this area.

While Sabbath suggests the theme of rest in the biblical narratives, there is much more to the story. In our present-day culture, we often think about rest as unwinding from work so that we can recover for more work. But in the biblical story, rest is also a time of reflection and celebration.

Moreover, Sabbath is oriented towards God and is a way to be with God. Or to put this somewhat differently, Sabbath is a space where we disconnect from normal duties in order to be present to ourselves in the presence of God. This is good for us, since stopping normal activity—taking a break—is refreshing and can lead us to new insights.

A Sabbath Spirituality

On this beautiful autumn morning in Brisbane, I am stopping to have some Sabbath moments—not to ask God for insights about what I am presently writing, but to make an *open* space. I am also moving out of my study to a spot in the garden.

But first I have to chase away a scrub turkey who is ruining part of the garden. These protected creatures know how to undo a newly planted garden bed in just a few minutes. That done, I simply pray, "Here I am, Lord, your wounded and seeking servant. Grant me grace and the blessing of your Spirit."

For a long time now, I have used the practice of *disengagement* in order to practice one dimension of Sabbath spirituality. While I am writing this at home, it is also possible to do this in the workplace.

Just stand up from your desk for one minute. Or walk to the water dispenser or the toilet. Or set aside ten minutes in your lunch break. Or make spaces for a Sabbath rest while riding the bus or train to or from work.

Clearly, this spirituality has nothing to do with rules. There is no thundering *must* from heaven. But it does have to do with a way of *being* in daily life. In some sense, it is seeking to be like the monks in a small way. They have their set times during the day for liturgical worship and prayer. During my day, in some small way, I can do the same.

While you may have your own reasons for making space for Sabbath rest, I will now tell you my reasons.

First, I feel an inner call or urge to make space for this rest. The call does not come from some great disciplinarian, but a loving friend. The call sounds something like this: *come and be with me.* I find this an attractive call for several reasons. It focuses on my relationship with the God who has stooped down in Christ and is present through the Spirit. Thus the call is about community and nurture. God is not first and foremost a great demander, but an encourager—and I need all the support I can get in this precarious journey of life. Because I want the Spirit to guide me, the call is also about gaining new perspectives and directives. It is easy for me to get lost in the midst of my much-doing or for me to keep doing my own thing. While seeking God's will may seem like a heavy call, it is far more difficult for me to live under the captaincy of my own fickle ways.

A second reason that I nurture a Sabbath spirituality is that I need moments of downtime. I work hard and tend to be driven, and so I often overextend myself. I need to stop from time to time, let go, and rest in a still place. I readily enter these moments in my hermitage of the heart.

The great surprise in all of this has been that my downtime is not characterized by fervent prayer or anxious knocking at heaven's door, but by stillness and receptivity, which has often been creative and insightful. Part of my Sabbath time takes place early in the morning, while it is still dark, and often thoughts come that help orient my day and what I am working on, whether teaching, writing, or various forms of social action. During this quiet and dark morning time, I am often given both encouragement and inspiration. This input springs up like a well from within me and makes it much easier for me to enter into the rest of the day—no matter how difficult it may seem.

Small forms of Sabbath during the day are important for me because they remind me of several important dimensions of human existence. First, we are all more than workers. Work is important, but so are rest and creativity. Work should not define who we are, for we are also lovers and dreamers who long for more.

Second, Sabbath is a powerful reminder that the entire created world—all forms of life—and our social existence need to be still and rest in order to recover. The season of winter exemplifies this, along with fallow land. The very rhythm of our day—moving from wakefulness and activity to sleep—also exemplifies a Sabbath spirituality.

I was brought up in a world where Sunday was a day of rest. All the shops were closed, and many citizens of my hometown went to church. That older world has long disappeared. In our 24/7 urban world, we have to set aside our own spaces for reflection and prayer. We need to foster Sabbath spirituality as a discipline that is sourced by the grace of God and the empowering Spirit.

20

Spiritual Midwifery

WHEN I WAS YOUNGER, I held a form of Christian activism that depended too much on what I, along with others, could do. Though we somewhat naively believed that we could change a lot in the world, our confidence was grounded in the work of the Spirit among us through our witness, service, and hospitality to the world.

Though we did achieve some things, we also experienced many internal and external setbacks and disappointments. Our early enthusiasm was dented, and we had to wrestle with discouragement.

Over the years, we came to see more clearly that we were not so much working *for* God, but *with* God. This meant that we had to become more reflective and prayerful. The ministry that was born out of discernment became more strategic than the ministry that had been born out of our enthusiasm. Along with this discovery, I had a growing sense that we were becoming *midwives* in the purposes of God for our world.

Midwives play an important role in the birthing process by assisting the mother and child at a particular point in time. Midwives are not the key players on the stage, for those roles belong to the mother and child.

In our witness and service with God, we are not the key players either. Instead, the focus is on what God through the Spirit is seeking to do in the life of another person or persons. We are merely midwives, assistants to the Holy Spirit.

Thus our challenge is to learn to practice midwifery. Obviously, a midwife does not bring about a pregnancy, and the baby is not the midwife's creation. The midwife assists the mother and prepares the setting for the birth to take place. The midwife focuses on the well-being of the mother, using the best procedures so that the baby may arrive safely in the world. The midwife also provides aftercare for the mother and newborn child.

This metaphor illuminates our task in the world. We can't bring about a new convert. Rather, God is at work, and it is our privilege to work with God in preparing for new life and aiding God's renewing and healing work in the world. We also have a role to play in providing aftercare.

The hermitage of the heart assumes that I am involved in my "normal" life of family, work, study, recreation, and other activities that bring me in contact with others. My work is to bring my hermitage of the heart into these situations. For this hermitage is not a place, but an inner disposition, an inner "life" that can be expressed as midwifery.

This means that, first and foremost, I need to enter life with an open and attentive gaze to what is happening around me. Through this basic lens, I can see that what is happening may not be on my agenda. Because we tend to be focused and preoccupied with our own issues and projects, this lens helps me be attentive to what lies outside of my direct gaze and interest.

The art of being attentive has key internal dimensions. First, there is the prayer, *Lord, what do I need to see?* Then there is a further prayer, *Lord, help me be open to interruption and being sidetracked.* In these prayers, we are seeking the Spirit's guidance.

When it is clear who or what we need to engage, we invite the Spirit to help us gaze on that person or situation with the eyes of faith and love. This work is preparatory and lies at the heart of spiritual midwifery. Under the guidance of the gentle Spirit, we are seeking to see something good come into being. We hoping for a gift to be given, a change to occur.

While we are engaged in this gentle, preparatory work, we are also standing *aside*. We do not push our agendas—no matter how good or necessary we might think they are. Nor are we overly interventionist, trying to force something to happen. This is a challenge, because we tend to have a "fix-it" mentality. We want to help—but in our way.

By standing aside, we create a *waiting* space between ourselves and the person we are engaging with our attention and love, just as a midwife prepares for the birth and then waits until the baby is ready to come into the world. In this waiting space, an insight, encouragement, or gift might emerge. Something is born!

This concept is by no means unique. Ignatian spirituality draws on a hermitage of heart, inviting us to see God in the things, persons, and events around us, and then beckons us to take that vision into the marketplace. Ignatian spiritual directors also know a lot about spiritual midwifery.

This is a wonderful and refreshing way to engage others. It is not a passive approach, where we just let things be, but a gentle engagement that exemplifies the kind of relationship we are meant to have with God the Spirit. We are neither trying to do our own thing in the face of an "absent" God, nor are we trying to fix things on God's behalf.

When we become midwives in the purposes of God for our world, we understand that God the Spirit is the main actor, who is at work in people's lives and in the world. We watch for the Spirit's presence and then join in the birthing process. This does not suggest that ministry to others is easy, for like midwifery, it is real work. But we understand our role as assistants, knowing that God alone through the Holy Spirit can bring new life.

21

The Invitation of Franciscan Spirituality

WHILE THE GIFT AND maintenance of a hermitage of the heart is a deeply personal matter, we can't live the Christian life well if our efforts are solo. The Christian faith journey is lived in relationship with Father, Son, and Holy Spirit, the communion of saints, society, and the created order. Thus relationality and interdependence comprise the core infrastructure of what it means to be human and a person of faith.

While seeking to be a follower of Christ, I have sought inspiration and encouragement from fellow travelers in the faith journey.[1] These companions, along with many others, have helped me build a hermitage of the heart.

One companion, St. Francis (1181–1226), has particularly challenged me during the latter half of my faith journey. As we get older, we tend to become more prosaic and conservative, and so Francis has helped to shake me up a bit!

I have been in contact with the Franciscan Brothers in Brisbane since the early 1970s, when I took retreats at their center, and

---

1. I have written meditational readers on Dietrich Bonhoeffer, Henri Nouwen, Jacques Ellul, Mother Teresa, Martin Luther King Jr., and Thomas Merton, who each, in turn, were my "companions" during an extended period of reading, reflection, and writing. From them, I received much encouragement.

we shared a common ministry of working with young people in the juvenile justice system.

Since that time, St. Francis remained at the periphery of my spiritual and missional concerns. Then later in life, I experienced a growing longing to explore the life, spirituality, and mission of Francis more fully.

During this period of exploration, six reoccurring themes kept coming to the fore. First, Francis retained a central focus on the Trinity. Second, Francis had a deep fascination with the incarnation and following Christ. Third, Francis loved the church and longed for its renewal. Fourth, Francis was committed to serving the poor. Fifth, Francis celebrated the beauty of creation. Sixth, Francis sensed that God could and would reveal himself/herself in the most unlikely places.

I was also fascinated and intrigued by the dialectical and creative tensions that Francis's life and ministry exhibited, particularly the following: he combined a high Trinitarian theology with a most lowly incarnation; he was committed both to mother church and to starting a missional community; he was devoted to a life of service as well as prayer; and he held a vision of a God of transcendent majesty alongside the God displayed through the created world.

Around this time, my close friend, Terry Gatfield, who had become a Franciscan Tertiary, unobtrusively challenged me to probe the ways of Francis more deeply. Thus the journey of formation began under the guidance of my mentor, Bronwyn Fryar, which eventually resulted in my becoming a Franciscan Tertiary (*tssf*) in 2014. Since then, Francis and the rich resources of Franciscan spirituality have been an inspiration. Here, I will focus on three major themes.[2]

---

2. Elsewhere I have explored the theme of peacemaking. See Ringma, "Franciscan Peacemaking."

A Mysticism of Motherhood

The Franciscan scholar Ilia Delio highlights how Franciscan spirituality does not ask the question, "what would Jesus do?," but rather, "how does Jesus live in me?"[3] Thus the central concern is how Christ is taking form and shape in our life. Put somewhat differently, Francis was concerned with becoming another Christ by conforming to the crucified Christ. Thus Christ is not simply our example, but our very being.

Delio points out that if the birthing of Christ in us is central, then "to become a spiritual mother is what imitation is all about."[4] This means that the Christian, as formed by Christ, is to live the spiritual mysticism of motherhood, which is to bring Christ to birth in others. Delio writes, "The goal of prayer is bringing Christ to birth."[5]

Francis birthed the Franciscan orders and a distinctive Christian spirituality. Francis birthed a vision of the created world that was resplendent with the glory of God. Francis birthed a vision of peacemaking and service to the poor.

Reflecting on the life of Francis in my hermitage of the heart left me with the following question: *At this point in my life, what is it that I am being called, in conformity with Christ, to birth in the world?* I think the answer to this is straightforward: *more birthing prayer, less talking and doing.*

Rebuilding and Renewal

I have long been fascinated by renewal movements in the life of the church. Over time, I have come to the basic conclusion that renewal movements only renew an aspect of the faith community and soon revert back to more conservative dimensions. This does not mean that change should not be attempted, but that those who work for change should be less pretentious.

---

3. Delio, *Franciscan Prayer*, 147.
4. Delio, *Franciscan Prayer*, 150.
5. Delio, *Franciscan Prayer*, 153.

The Invitation of Franciscan Spirituality

One of the things that has fascinated me about Francis was his central call to "rebuild my [God's] house."[6] He began to engage this work practically and specifically by rebuilding the ruins of the church at San Damiano. Yet as he began to obey this simple and specific call, wider dimensions of his call began to emerge. This is frequently the case. We need only think of Mother Teresa's simple call to do something beautiful for God in serving the poorest of the poor or Jean Vanier's call to learn to live together with those with disabilities and trace how those particular calls subsequently unfolded and guided their lives. Francis's call to rebuild a specific church building led him to form a religious missional order, which eventually blessed and renewed "mother" church.

As the Franciscan scholar Michael Crosby has pointed out, Francis's concept of *oikos* (house) led to a growing vision of *oikonomia* (the shape and economics of society).[7] This meant that Francis was not only concerned about the church, but the whole world, and his concern about the sociopolitical order was connected with his love for the natural world, which sustains life itself. As Crosby summarizes, "Francis saw creation and everyone and everything in it [as] part of God's domain or household."[8]

You might well wonder what this has to do with a hermitage of the heart. The answer is: everything. While a hermitage of the heart is particular, it is not narrow. It is a broad place, for it seeks to carry, in a small way, the concerns of the reign of God for the whole world.

A Spirituality of Wonder

Giovanni di Fidanza Bonaventure (1221–1274), an early Franciscan theologian who became the Minister General of the Franciscan order, has encouraged and challenged me to embrace a spirituality

---

6. Crosby, *Finding Francis, Following Christ*, 52.
7. Crosby, *Finding Francis, Following Christ*, 56.
8. Crosby, *Finding Francis, Following Christ*, 57.

of wonder. With my more pragmatic orientation, this has been a big shift!

My Friesian cultural background and upbringing in the Reformed faith meant that I drank in the Protestant work ethic along with my mother's milk. This ethic impacted both my involvement in secular work and Christian ministry. If there was anything I needed to learn, it was a spirituality of Sabbath and an ability to gaze and wonder.

Francis has helped me learn this through his nature mysticism, and Bonaventure has helped to articulate this vision for me:

Open your eyes, alert the ears of your spirit, open your lips and apply your heart so that in all creatures you may see, hear, praise, love and worship, glorify and honor your God.[9]

Here is an invitation to live with openness and wonder—not only in relation to spiritual things, but in relation to everything. This is harder to do than we realize, for in the West we continue to be marked by all sorts of dualisms. To see all things in relation to the presence and glory of God is to live with a newfound joy.

This sense of gazing in wonderment does not mean that everything merges into an undesignated oneness. Bonaventure describes "the soul's deep affection . . . centered in God and transformed, as it were, into him," and suggests that for this to take place, "then ask grace, not learning; desire, not understanding; the groanings of prayer, not industry in study . . ."[10]

This suggests new ways of knowing. Though I have spent over thirty years in postgraduate education and see the value of scholarly formation, I also know that more is needed to light a flame at the core of our very being. This light is the power of grace framed in a Christo-mysticism.

I am deeply grateful for the gift of this life-giving spiritual tradition. To further whet your appetite, I will close with some wisdom from Francis.

Where there is charity and wisdom

---

9. Quoted in Ringma, *Hear the Ancient Wisdom*, 33.
10. Quoted in Ringma, *Hear the Ancient Wisdom*, 124.

there is neither fear nor ignorance.[11]

Inwardly cleansed, interiorly enlightened, and inflamed by the fire of the Holy Spirit may we be able to follow in the footprints of Your beloved Son.[12]

Praised be You, my Lord, with all your creatures . . . Brother Sun . . . Sister Moon . . . Brother Wind . . . Sister Water . . . Brother Fire . . . [and] our Sister Mother Earth who sustains and governs us.[13]

Therefore, let us desire nothing else
let us wish for nothing else
let nothing else please us and cause us delight
except our Creator and Redeemer and Savior.[14]

11. Armstrong and Brady, trans., *The Complete Works of Francis and Clare*, 35.

12. Armstrong and Brady, trans., *The Complete Works of Francis and Clare*, 61.

13. Armstrong and Brady, trans., *The Complete Works of Francis and Clare*, 39.

14. Armstrong and Brady, trans., *The Complete Works of Francis and Clare*, 133.

22

Prayer and Protest

WHILE LIVING IN A monastery or spending time in a hermitage does involve a measure of withdrawal from ordinary life, a hermitage of the heart is not about inward piety or withdrawing from the "big, bad world." Rather, a hermitage of the heart is about cultivating sacred spaces and practices in the midst of daily life.

The challenge for those who are living a monastic life is how to remain in touch with the burdens of the world so they can carry them in prayer. My challenge is how to maintain a hermitage of the heart and to continue to pray while I am engaged in the affairs of daily life, with so much demanding my attention and concern and so much to do in service of the common good.

In our service of the common good, our challenge as Christians is not only to enhance and bless *what is,* but also to critique it and to live toward a vision of *what could be* in the reign of God. Thus the Christian presence in the world is not simply about maintenance, but also about transformation.

This leads to a discussion about the relationship between prayer and protest. I believe that both have a place in the Christian task in the church and world. Yet whenever I have been involved in protests, I have suffered consequences from both Christians and those who hold power in society. The former have charged that such action disrespects God's constituted civil power. The latter have labeled me as a communist, which has led to further rejection by the faith community. All of this has been painful and difficult, and it has led me to think more carefully about the relationship between prayer and protest.

Prayer is not, first and foremost, about bringing my needs to God or asking God to bless my "bucket list." Instead, prayer is about entering into a relational space, where we are invited and drawn by the Spirit into the presence of God in order to listen and be attentive to the Spirit.

In this relational space, the God of the biblical narratives—who is both a redeemer and a just God with a heart for the poor—will inevitably remind us of the needs of the world. This reminder will inevitably call us to respond to the issues of our time by working and living towards renewal and transformation, because God's passion is for the healing and renewal of all things.

Despite the incessant proclamations from secular culture, God is not a delusion, nor has God abandoned the world. Rather, God is present with us and invites us to share God's concern for the world and all it contains.

You may ask, "Doesn't sharing in God's concern for the world simply call us to pray, love, and serve?" Of course! But loving and serving God may also call us to be prophetic—which can involve protest.

Abraham Heschel, the famous twentieth-century rabbi, did not merely philosophize about the importance of engaging the "other" in his quest for justice. He also joined Martin Luther King Jr. in his civil disobedience and protest movement. In the long march from Selma to Montgomery, Heschel exclaimed, "my [marching] feet are doing the praying."

Thus, in attending to God, we are also attending to our neighbors, and in attending to our neighbors, we are also attending to God. Said differently, prayer is not only about being in the chapel, but also about being on the road, joining the long march for justice.

I have been involved in various protest movements, and I can't imagine sustaining this long march without spiritual resources.

The hermitage of the heart is such a resource, providing an abiding spiritually that is rooted in daily life.

In considering this, several things stand out. First and foremost, protest is an act of love. It is not motivated by hate or the quest for power, but by a great love for our country, which stirs us to point out its faults even while recognizing our own. This means that we need to be willing to stand up to the cause of making things right, which will cost us a lot—maybe even our life.

Second, protest is an act of incarnation and humiliation as we follow the Prince of Peace, Jesus Christ, into the world.

Third, protest is an act of prayer as we trust that through God's Spirit, righteousness, shalom, and justice will blossom in places of darkness and oppression.

Fourth, protest not only seeks to point out what is wrong, but also to champion a new vision for the way ahead. Because protest dreams that things can be more just, protest risks a peaceful confrontation of "the powers"—the political, social, and economic structures that are meant to serve the common good, but have become self-seeking and oppressive.

Moreover, protest not only seeks to aid the oppressed, but also to "convert" the oppressor. In the tradition of Gandhi and Martin Luther King Jr., those who protest dearly want an unjust government to "see the light" and to turn things around. Protestors in this tradition are not calling for a utopia, but a return to the pathways of goodness that build well-being for all of creation and extend compassion and hospitality to the needy.

Since prayer and protest belong to the hermitage of the heart, such a hermitage will not only be a place for quiet meditation, but also a place of struggle for life.

23

Yearning

As I write this, I am crying, which I am doing a lot lately—and even more since I spent time at the hermitage. I don't think that I am crying because I am getting older and becoming more sentimental. I am just not "wired" that way.

But talking about what I yearn for does bring me close to the core of whom I am, for I don't think we are defined so much by what we think about and do, but by our longings.

Some people may think that once we come to faith in Christ, live that out over many years, and have the hope of a life to come in God's final future, we have nothing to long for anymore. We have "arrived," so to speak.

But I believe this is a serious misunderstanding of the faith journey. Yearnings and longings don't cease when we come to faith. Rather, they increase and become even more painful.

My longings have little to do with comfort and security. I am not longing for a Ferrari or a home near the beach. My yearnings, which often cause me pain, have to do with what is happening in our world in the light of God's good news, the message of shalom, and God's vision for a world of justice and human well-being.

I am pained by the way we do politics and business, and conduct ourselves towards others, particularly strangers and the needy. We seem to be promoting a way of life that does not build a world where the whole of creation can flourish. Sadly, the misuse of power and privilege is alive and well in our world, where the politics of isolationism rather than a spirituality of hospitality seems to be the order of the day.

My own failure to be more deeply shaped by the gospel causes me the most pain. The self-referential world we are shaping, particularly in the West, is a candidate for all forms of idolatry, for when we become self-made gods, we are accountable to no one.

You may well be tuning out on this reflection if you think my viewpoint is negative and pessimistic. You may want to challenge me by pointing to all the scientific and cultural progress that we have made in the modern world—and I would hasten to agree, for we are living with better healthcare, and we have many other benefits in our affluent world.

However, though I may benefit from all that science and technology have brought to us, this does not decrease my pain—but increases it. For one, these benefits are not available for all of humanity. We live in a world that is still deeply divided by "haves and have-nots." Anyone who has spent time in the majority (non-Western) world knows the dehumanizing face of poverty.

Moreover, our prosperity has not spiritually enriched us. Instead, we seem to be more "hollow," demanding, and less compassionate than ever. Inwardly rootless, transcendentally absent, morally derelict, we have become the restless "wanderers" in our modern urban-scape. Again, anyone who returns to the West after working in the majority world can sense this.

So I do not think I am a pessimist. Rather, I am deeply hopeful, but I can't be hopeful without knowing the pain of what is not—but could be.

For by hoping—and praying and working—towards what is possible under the grace and reign of God, we experience pain and distress whenever we come up against the absence of that possibility. This wakes us up to the painful reminder that we can't bring about the unfolding of God's purposes in our time, no matter how hard we work, how much we pray, or how deep our longing might be. So we are called to live as watchers for what God will *yet* do.

As a watcher and waiter, what do I yearn for? Most basically, I long to see the day when the Spirit of God is more active in the church and the world. Having seen some inklings of this in the charismatic movement and the Jesus revolution many decades ago, I am not longing for a repetition, but a movement that will be far more deeply rooted, one that will be sustained much longer so that renewal will be more lasting.

This does not mean that I expect all people to become Christians. But I do long for all people to have a spiritual anchor point, to be gracious to others, to be forgiving, and to work for the common good, where peace and justice can flourish.

Obviously, my longings far outstrip our present-day realities. My yearnings seem so far out of reach, and this continues to give me a lot of anguish. But I won't abandon these dreams—not simply because I am a stubborn Dutchman and a Friesian to boot, but because I believe that they are close to the heart of God.

God, in Christ, has made a way to redeem all humanity. God's purpose is for the well-being of the whole world in the shalom of God. God is passionate about the flourishing of justice. God's heart is for the poor.

In the hermitage of the heart, I long for God's heartbeat to become my heartbeat. I often feel the heartache of God. I worry about the long-term personal and social consequences for how we have pushed God to the periphery of our existence. We have lost far more than personal piety. We have lost the very basis of our existence, which is to worship our Creator God, embrace the God who redeems and heals us, and devote our lives to the service of the God of all grace. How tragic it is that we—who have been created in God's image and likeness—have so diminished ourselves!

24

Identifying with Jesus

THERE ARE HUGE PRESSURES in our world *not* to be too reflective. The mantra we hear constantly is that we need to be "connected" and productive. This mantra keeps us doing whatever we are doing without reflecting seriously about its value, purpose, or effectiveness. Living this way, we become increasingly busy and uncritical.

If we are to build a hermitage of the heart, we need to nurture a reflective interiority. The intention is not to create an inner vacuum of tranquility, but a sensitive discernment.

To discern what is true, good, beautiful, and just, we need a dynamic ethical framework. We must first be able to identify our guiding values, and from within that framework, we can identify with certain causes and issues.

My core values are not grounded, first and foremost, in certain principles, but in a relationship with the God who is Father, Son, and Holy Spirit. I seek to live in the joy of celebrating the Creator God and to see all things as reflecting something of God's glory. I rejoice in the gift of salvation and healing that Christ brings. I seek to be open to the ever-brooding and renewing Spirit.

Out of the beauty of this relationship, I seek to learn more about God's ways with us by reading the biblical narratives, participating in the faith community, and engaging our world.

While I seek to learn from all of Scripture, I am particularly drawn to the Old Testament prophetic writings and the New Testament Gospels, as they inspire me with a vision of God as a healer and restorer who is seeking to bring shalom to all. They also inspire me to believe that God's action in the world seeks to call the powerful to practice justice and to uplift the poor in their struggles for life. The heartbeat of all this is the invitation to live in the embrace of God's love for all.

By participating in the faith community, I am constantly reminded of God's good news and nourished through worship, word, sacrament, and fellowship. The faith community "holds" me within its tradition. Or to put that more intimately, the church is the mother of my faith and holds me to its bosom for nurture and support.

By engaging the world, I am everywhere reminded of the goodness of God in creation, which includes the human community. There are signs everywhere that speak of bountiful provision and human kindness and concern. At the same time, there are also the marks of exploitation, neglect, exclusion, oppression, abuse, and dehumanization.

Because the world is constantly mirroring this sense of conflict, the movement of grace is often met with a prevailing and distorted worldliness that does not lead to well-being and justice.

Thus I seek, however partially, to identify with the biblical vision of well-being for the whole world and to identify particularly with victims of oppression and exclusion. But I do so with much shame because my identification with both the gospel and those who are needy is often so piecemeal and skimpy.

I am far too selfish and self-protective to live the gospel fully. To help me live the gospel more closely, I became a Franciscan tertiary some years ago. In this way, I seek to identify myself with St. Francis as well as Jesus.

I have been drawn to the Franciscan life because it makes more concrete and practical the things that I already believe and seek to practice. This includes a love for God the Creator and the beauty of the created world. It also involves a dual call "to build my church" and to serve the poor. It highlights that the grace of God can be found in the most unlikely places, such as kissing a leper. It also emphasizes the task of peacemaking in our world and calls us to be seed-bearers of the kingdom of God, bringing forth fruit that enhances life and the flourishing of the whole world.

While some may not want to identify with any ideology, group, or cause so that they can be completely self-determining, I think that is not a wise way to live. First, being part of a group or movement does not dent our personal identity. After all, we choose to join and cooperate. Second, joining with others in a common cause helps us move beyond ourselves into something bigger. Our self-constructed "world" is far too small. We need to have the inner maturity to be stretched by others. Third, if we wish to bring about changes in our world, then we have to join with others. Tragically, in the work of social transformation, groups are often so divided that they can only bring about the "fractured" change that characterizes them.

This means that identification with something beyond ourselves is an important dimension of living well. I am not a solo hero. My discernment needs to be tested in community. My values and concerns need to be much larger than anything I can orchestrate. The vision of the reign of God that is embodied in the person and work of Christ and perpetuated by the Spirit engenders reconciliation and healing, peacemaking and community-building, justice and well-being. Surely this is a big enough orchestral score to keep me "playing" till the end of my days!

In this time of political correctness, with our tendency to reduce one another to our lowest common denominator, we may feel ashamed to identify with Christians. Yet should we be ashamed to be a people who are seeking to follow the suffering, healing Christ into the world? Should we be ashamed to seek the well-being of the poor? Certainly not!

While we can rightly point to the sins of the church in history, and while some can rightly accuse me of failure and hypocrisy, we can't find much wrong with the Christ of the Gospels. For me, at least, he is my example rather than Marx.

Where I fail, I am responsible, so blame me for tarnishing the good name of Jesus, the Galilean, but don't blame him. Have another look at the one who took upon himself the madness of our world in order to usher in its redemption and renewal.

Do you really want to change the world? Then don't rely on the power of our social and political institutions alone. Identify with Jesus, who identified with the poor and downtrodden, and seek to work out his transformation in the world through the power of the Spirit.

25

Liminality

THE HERMITAGE OF THE heart is not a place of shining clarity, but more of a safe place to see things darkly, as in a smudged mirror.

You may be surprised that I regard a dark place as safe, but that is because anyone who claims to have all the light is dangerous. Such people gain guru status, become larger than life, and eventually become controlling or even despotic.

The Christian life is marked by humility. We are on a journey. We have only touched the outer edges of Christ's garment. We live by faith, and in hope we move forward. But the fullness of light has not yet come, and so we continue to seek, pray, and long for greater participation in the life of God in Christ.

By "dark" place, I do not mean a place of evil or fear, but an in-between or transitional space, a place of liminality.

Liminality is experiential, a sort of no-man's land, where previous certainties have collapsed, and new certainties have not yet swum into view. In liminality, we experience a kind of existential paradigm shift.

We may experience this during the aging process, a time of ecological crisis, war, a relationship breakdown, or after a major health crisis or a bruising betrayal. The causes are endless, but the effect we feel is that we've been thrown off our perch, as if the ground under our feet is in upheaval. For a time, everything—including our faith—seems shattered.

In the journey of faith, these experiences that bruise us also challenge us to embrace the "dark" night of the soul. More basically, these difficult experiences invite us to walk a "new" road with God, a *via dolorosa*—the painful road of following the suffering Christ. This is a road of waiting, mystery, and uncertainty through an in-between place, with all its fermenting anxieties and fragile hopes.

I have walked this road a number of times, particularly in cross-cultural work and after some major health breakdowns. I am thankful for the ways these experiences have enriched my life.

One major lesson I have learned is that life and the journey of faith cannot be lived in perpetual equilibrium, for there are always transition points and conversions.

But God is present in these transitional spaces in a new way—one marked by mystery, waiting, and surprise. Because of this, we must firmly resist the urge to dash quickly to new certainties or to grab hold of something solid to fill the empty space. Rather, when we enter a liminal space, we must wait to see what God will do in God's time and God's way.

This means that the hermitage of the heart can be a difficult place of struggle and uncertainty. Thus the hermitage of the heart is a place for pilgrims.

We can extend the concept of liminality from the personal sphere to the communal and corporate dimensions of life and society. For example, the present-day church in the West could be seen as a liminal space. With the collapse of Christendom, the Enlightenment's critique of the church, the decrease in membership in churches in the West, and the ongoing marginalization of the church in society, there are many indications that the church is in an in-between space. The "power and the glory" of Christendom has faded. What will the new future of the church in the West look like?

I think these circumstances are good for the church, as perhaps something much more credible will emerge. Out of the ashes of the old, new forms of the church and its practices and mission may agonize their way into being.

Rather than charting the way forward with all our certainties intact—many of which were born out of our insecurities—we can approximate the logic and practices of the Desert Fathers and Mothers. While their liminality was forged after Christianity began to gain imperial status (and thereby to lose its distinctive nature), the present-day church is also finding itself in a liminal space as it is being pushed out of the public sphere. Both circumstances suggest a serious weakening of the influence of the church in the world.

Does this mean that we are being called—like our desert forebears—into new spaces of prayer and reflection in order to re-engage our world in new ways? This may well be so. We may be called to inhabit places of retreat even more in order to seek the face of God for the renewal of the world.

While going on a weekend retreat is valuable, it is not always doable. Thus we need to build hermitages of the heart, where we cultivate spaces for Sabbath spirituality in our homes, places of work, churches, and in the midst of all the spheres of life.

This means that we need to learn to stop, desist, lay down our tools, turn off our communication devices, and turn our faces to become more attentive to God. This is not about us finding God, but God finding us. We need to be willing to hear, and we also need to desire to do what God wants.

This hermitage of the heart is a gift and a practice that is forged out of our love of God and neighbor. The hermitage of the heart is the "engine room" of all we seek to be and do for the purposes of the reign of God. While we may wander far from this hermitage at times, its very emptiness will beckon us to return.

26

The Invitation of Ignatian Spirituality

DURING MY LATE TEENS and early twenties, I was involved in theological studies and came across St. Ignatius of Loyola (c. 1495–1556) in my church history courses. In that setting, I saw Ignatius as a reformer within the Roman Catholic church.

Many years later, while teaching in Manila and through contact with Father Thomas Green, a spiritual director and author, St. Ignatius became more important to me. Later still, my evangelical friends in Brisbane who were involved in spiritual formation drew heavily on Ignatian spirituality.

I have come to appreciate how the all-embracing vision of Ignatian spirituality is important for a hermitage of the heart, particularly its emphasis on the Lordship of God, a contemplative posture, and the presence of God in the whole gamut of life. Its central mantra of being contemplatives in action is birthed by following Christ through obedience, which has its genesis in the beautiful awareness that, first and foremost, God does not give us gifts, but his very self. As a response to this gratuitous nature of God, we are called to give our very self to Christ.

Following are some key themes in Ignatian spirituality that are particularly helpful for the hermitage of the heart.

Heart Matters: The Examined Life

In order to follow Christ as our greatest love and obey his call to serve the world, we need a sustaining spirituality. A key emphasis of Ignatian spirituality is on spiritual exercises and retreats. Ignatian spirituality sees the heart as the motivational center of our being, and so a core question is, "What are the movements of God in your heart?"

We can come to an awareness of God's movements in our heart in multiple ways: reading the gospel and placing ourselves in the story, engaging in spiritual direction, and using a range of reflective practices to gain insight into what the Spirit is seeking to bring to our attention—not only for ourselves, but also for others and the realities of our world.

One reflective practice in Ignatian spirituality is doing "the examen" at the end of each day. The logic of this practice is as follows. First, we give thanks to God for the blessings of the day. Second, we ask for the enlightening presence of the Holy Spirit. Third, we review the day in terms of its "life-giving" realities and its "death-dealing" experiences. Fourth, we express sorrow for our sin and failure and seek God's grace and forgiveness. Fifth, we give ourselves anew to the God of love, who embraces and holds us in his/her grace. Sixth, we reflect on the following questions: "What has Christ done for us on the cross?" and "What does our sin do to Jesus and others?"

As a reflective spirituality, Ignatian spirituality is important to a hermitage of the heart, particularly its emphasis on the *examined life* rather than a life taken for granted.

Pilgrimage: A Missional Spirituality

The Christian life is a journey of faith and obedience that each of us have to make, but we have many companions on the way. Ignatian spirituality seeks to guide the pilgrim on this journey.

Ignatian wisdom is rooted in the understanding that Jesus Christ came to serve the world, and he beckons all who seek to follow him to be with him, think like him, and act like him. This calls the Christian pilgrim to be attentive constantly to God and to the ways that the Spirit is working in the world. Within this contemplative posture of attentiveness, the pilgrim asks what Christ wants the pilgrim to do. This posture connects contemplation with action. We are attentive in order to obey. Thus Ignatian spirituality is a *missional spirituality*, which means that a hermitage of the heart is never only an inward exercise, for Christ is both a shepherd who nurtures us and also a commander who gives us a task.

Discernment

The genesis of our work as contemplatives in action is discernment. We discern who Christ is and what Christ does. We discern what the Gospels invite us into and what they call us to do. We discern the movement of God in the depths of our desires and the hopes of our world.

One theme in this discernment process is the way we move between consolation and desolation. Consolation increases the life of faith, hope, and love. Desolation diminishes us. Consolation is life-giving; desolation is death-dealing.

Christ is the norm for this discernment process. Christ offers us life, but it is a life of discipleship that involves humility and service. The enemy of our souls, the *diabolus*, offers us the seemingly far more attractive gifts of riches and power.

This means that discernment is no walk in the park. The *diabolus*, the world, and our own foolish hearts entice us with attractive possibilities, whereas the invitation of Christ seems overly difficult—even impossible.

The hermitage of the heart creates space for reflection, which provides the setting for our discernment. But the heartbeat of our discernment is regulated by the Gospels, the Spirit, and our spiritual companions. St. Ignatius of Loyola is one such companion. Following is some of his wisdom.

> *There are "two ends [which] are complementary: union with God which is most intimate and total," and "a state of life in which [one] . . . can serve God best."*[1]
>
> *In this "interior consolation. . . to some persons [God] gives light, and to others [God] reveals many secrets."*[2]
>
> *Contemplate God our Lord as being present in every creature.*[3]
>
> *For he gave us an example that . .we might seek through the aid of [Christ's] grace to imitate and follow him, since he is the way which leads people to life.*[4]
>
> *Love ought to manifest itself more by deeds than by words.*[5]

There is much more to learn from this rich tradition, but in my journey of the hermitage of the heart, Ignatian spirituality helps me to see God at work everywhere—in the ordinary places of life and even in the most unlikely circumstances. As I continue on this journey, I need the consolations of the Spirit and a reflective attentiveness to lead me to true discernment.

---

1. Ganss, ed., *Ignatius of Loyola*, 390.
2. Ganss, ed., *Ignatius of Loyola*, 336.
3. Ganss, ed., *Ignatius of Loyola*, 133.
4. Ganss, ed., *Ignatius of Loyola*, 286.
5. Ganss, ed., *Ignatius of Loyola*, 176.

27

Life's "Curve Balls"

My life had been on a fairly even keel when I took six months away from ministry, research, writing, and family responsibilities to spend most of my time in a hermitage on my friend's bushland property. I still feel grateful to all who gave me this generous space to be quiet, reflect, and pray. My desire for this time at a hermitage was not the result of some crisis, but something I was simply longing to do.

As I have already noted,[1] nothing too "miraculous" happened during that time. The biggest surprise was how disorientated I was upon my re-entry and how difficult regular spiritual practices became for me.

Then major health issues threw further "curve balls" into my life. I was looking after a sick spouse, sick myself, and taking care of the house-related responsibilities—which all left me exhausted in every way. I felt as if I had literally fallen off my perch—and I am still recovering.

This raised some important issues in thinking about a hermitage of the heart. Clearly, this inner place cannot be cordoned off from the difficulties that inevitably come our way nor are we protected from what happens around us. Thus this inner state will be affected by our circumstances and health.

1. Ringma, *Sabbath Time*.

A Fragile Hope

My physical sickness and exhaustion wreaked havoc in my journey of a hermitage of the heart. Certain disciplines fell by the wayside. My emotional life turned gray. Spiritually, I entered "blah, blah" land.

None of this indicated that I had fallen out of God's hand or that God had turned his/her back on me. Nor was I experiencing a "dark night" of the soul. I was simply exhausted and somewhat depressed.

But I worried about all this, because it was not how I wanted to live. Being a fairly disciplined person, I felt "bad" about my spiritual state.

What complicated this even more was that I had made certain vows as a Franciscan tertiary (*tssf*) and a companion of the Northumbria Community (Brisbane) to commit to daily disciplines of reading, reflection, and prayer. But nearly all these disciplines went "out the window." With the time approaching to renew my Franciscan vows, I was in a dilemma about what to do. Surely, I couldn't renew my vows when I had been so far from fulfilling them over the previous six months.

On discussing this with my Franciscan companions and leadership, I was encouraged to renew my vows anyway, which I did with a great sense of joy and relief.

Since a hermitage of the heart has to do with a phenomenology of daily spirituality, let me reflect on this entire experience.

The Christian life is rooted in the love and grace of God in Christ, which is extended ever so freely and generously to each one of us. This is the fountain from which we are invited to drink for the whole of our lives.

At the same time, we are invited to respond to God in worship, friendship, and service. We are graced to participate in what God is doing to beautify and grow the kingdom of God and to renew the face of the earth. Thus while grace abounds, we are also called to participation and responsibility.

Yet we can easily get things out of balance when we assume that too much depends on us or that God and others will not be generous when we are weak and struggling. We should not be surprised by any of this.

We may have been brought up to see our identity in terms of our achievements instead of being rooted in the love of God. We may see God as demanding or sense that the Christian life and our service depends on us. After all, we don't see many of the New Testament miracles in our churches and lives!

Western culture reinforces these ideas by celebrating productivity and success—even if that success is merely based on the number of Facebook "friends" and Twitter "likes" we have. Even in the church, failures tend to be quickly overlooked.

The church has also been infected by this kind of thinking. We gather as a community of those who are doing well under the blessing of God, and we share praise to God, but we don't share our needs and failures. Unlike the early Church Fathers, we don't see salvation as medicine nor the gathered church as a hospital for restoration and healing.

The great New Testament theme of the risen and ascended Christ, in whom and for whom all things hold together, is that he is the Lamb that was slain.

There is much in life that can overwhelm us, especially as the forces of nature become more and more threatening, and so we need to learn to see ourselves in a different light. As Westerners, we tend to see ourselves as controlling, with the power to shape the environment and more or less govern the world. As Western Christians, we continue to see ourselves as the major shapers of global Christianity (even though this is rapidly changing).

In light of these big-picture realities—and my small experience of illness and difficulty—our challenge is to develop a very different posture towards God and one another.

Our elitism, self-sufficiency, "prosperity" gospel, and do-goodism may need to be replaced by a very different spiritual gestalt. Maybe our self-reliance needs to be replaced by a far greater dependency on God? Rather than merely being busy, perhaps we need to become more prayerful? Rather than championing our abilities, maybe we need to become more vulnerable? Maybe we should focus on the journey rather than arriving? Maybe the gospel needs to focus on the "weakness" of God rather the triumphant, conquering God? Maybe?

As of now, I am grateful for these difficult months—and thankful that I could renew my Franciscan vows.

28

A Fragile Hope

As you have made your way through these pages, you probably will have noted that I am not a happy optimist. Nor am I a sober pessimist. I like to see myself as a realist who is marked by hope. Whether I live this well is another story. There is always a gap between one's beliefs and self-awareness and how one acts in the world.

But in building a hermitage of the heart, the role of hope is crucial. In fact, hope is essential to being able to live well with ourselves and others. This means that we have to hope both for self-improvement and for a better world. To hope only for the latter or the former is delusional.

It may be possible to say all of this more strongly. Hope is intrinsic to what it means to be human, and the loss of hope scars who we are meant to be, and will impact how we act towards others.

It is, therefore, not surprising that the topic of hope has been warmly discussed and debated in philosophical, sociological, and religious circles. In these circles, we find both negative and positive perspectives.

Some of the negative views may be summarized as follows. First, hope can function as a tardy excuse for laziness and poor planning and execution. Second, hope can function as mere wishful thinking and unhelpful irrationality. Third, hope can be seductive and make us believe fervently in false promises and messiahs. Fourth, hope can be counterproductive because it can agonizingly prolong the journey of disappointment.[1]

There are also many positive views, which include the following. First, hope means that there is a future. Second, what we hope for is usually what we will work towards. Third, hope anticipates betterment and human improvement. Fourth, hope creates a "productive anxiety" that moves us to new endeavors. Fifth, hope is marked by humility in that what we hope for is bigger than each of us. Sixth, hope is marked by fragility in that it is never cast in iron-clad guarantees, but only risk-taking enterprises.[2]

Within a Christian theological frame, hope is rooted in the action of God in Christ, through the empowering and renewing Spirit, to renew all things and bring them into the beautiful domain of God's final future, where shalom will come to its fullness and God will be the integrating center of all things.

Christian hope lives in the light of this glorious future and anticipates this future in a penultimate way. In other words, Christian hope is for pilgrims and dreamers, healers and prophets, who are living the "yet and the not-yet" of God's kingdom reign in the hope that God's continuing presence and grace will bless humanity, the earth, and the cosmos.

This "big-picture" hope continues to inspire and shape my involvement in the world, but my missional projects and service are not the source of my hope.

---

1. The grave of the Greek novelist Nikos Kazantzakis had these words inscribed on it: "I hope for nothing. I fear nothing. I am free," quoted in Rees, ed., *Brewer's Famous Quotations*, 264. George Bernard Shaw's famous quote is: "He [she] who has never hoped can never despair," quoted in Ratcliffe, ed., *The Oxford Dictionary of Thematic Quotations*, 185.

2. The American novelist and poet Marge Piercy comments on hope: "hope sleeps in our bones like a bear waiting for spring to rise and walk," quoted in Ratcliffe, ed., *Oxford Dictionary of Thematic Quotations*, 185. The English writer Dr. Samuel Johnson speaks of "the triumph of hope over experience," quoted in Rees, ed., *Brewer's Famous Quotations*, 259.

By way of example, I spent nearly twenty years working with street people and those with addiction issues, and I saw the drug abuse problem become worse, not better. Though some people were helped, and quite a number did come to faith, overall, the drug problem only escalated.

This means that our hope cannot be based on our effectiveness. It has to be based elsewhere. Like a tapestry with vivid colors, this "elsewhere" has several dimensions. First, hope is rooted in the grand narratives of the biblical story regarding what God has done and will do. Second, hope is inspired by our experience of the presence of God in healing, renewing, and restoring the world. Though these experiences may be small, they are significant. Third, hope gains its orientation through God's call upon our lives to serve in particular ways. Fourth, hope is nurtured in the faith community and through certain spiritual practices.

None of this means that there is something prosaic and predictable about living in hope. Hope is restless and leans beyond itself into the future. Hope does not simply accept what is, or how things are, but stubbornly longs for what can and should be.

The French sociologist and lay theologian Jacques Ellul expresses some of the restlessness and longing of Christian hope. First, hope is truly born in the midst of what is seemingly impossible. Second, hope does not add a little addendum—a little extra—to our knowing and acting. It is never "a dash of pepper or a spoonful of mustard" to our ability.[3] Third, hope looks forward to the plenitude—the fullness—of the "not-yet" nature of the reign or kingdom of God. Fourth, hope "is not self-fulfilment by one's own powers."[4] Fifth, hope has critical power because it refuses to accept the way things are in light of what they can be in the promises of God. Finally, hope calls us to enter into "conflict with God"[5] and to "protest before God"[6] by challenging God to act when what is wrong and unjust seems to prosper.

3. Ellul, *Hope in Time of Abandonment*, 201.
4. Ellul, *Hope in Time of Abandonment*, 189.
5. Ellul, *Hope in Time of Abandonment*, 179.
6. Ellul, *Hope in Time of Abandonment*, 180.

A Fragile Hope

In light of these summary statements, Ellul challenges us further. First, as Christians, we must never commit ourselves to "weary resignation."[7] Second, in the face of seemingly hopeless situations, we are invited to self-reflection and repentance. Third, the dynamic quality of hope is not to work ourselves into the ground, but to arouse God in light of God's character and promises. If God is a God of justice, and if injustice is flourishing, then we must "assail" God to act. We should also expect God to call us to cooperate with God's actions. Fourth, it is appropriate for hope to burn with a certain impatience for a fuller unveiling of the kingdom of God since "God will break through"[8] by God's word and work.

Finally, Christian hope cries out to God in the desert of our experience. In our institutional, national, and global circumstances, we refuse the claims of the "fallen powers" and reject the narratives of those who seek to justify their unjust practices. We also refuse to accept the seeming absence and powerlessness of God by proclaiming "that God is there" and God is the God who "saves and heals"[9]—not only those who are oppressed, but also the oppressors.

Thus Christian hope is rooted in God's final future, but also in the hope that God will intervene in the midst of "exploitation, dictatorships, and the universal destruction of nature."[10] If God acts in these ways, then we are called to be like God! This challenge is not a call to a crusade, but to be a healing presence in the world. God works through the mystery of the power of the cross and the life-giving Spirit. Thus our living and serving are cruciform, our hope is fragile, our prayers are marked by lament, and though our impact may be little, we will not give up our hope in God's love and concern for the world and its final completion in the purposes of God.

---

7. Ellul, *Hope in Time of Abandonment*, 183.
8. Ellul, *Hope in Time of Abandonment*, 208.
9. Ellul, *Hope in Time of Abandonment*, 216.
10. Ellul, *Hope in Time of Abandonment*, 213.

Afterword

THERE MAY BE STAGES in the Christian life, or the Christian life may be a pilgrimage, where we draw closer and closer to our destination of fullness of life. Or, as our ancient forebears suggested, we may be climbing a ladder towards greater fidelity and spirituality. Maybe!

But I think not! My journey over the past several years does not suggest any sort of progression or ladder-climbing. In fact, the opposite seems to be the case. Living the Christian life continues to be a journey fraught with all sorts of challenges, and this journey has nothing to do with progress, but is simply marked by the grace of God, which continues to hold us in our times of joy, seasons of responsibility, the difficulties of life, and also our own stupidities.

Some of the most fundamental challenges of our journey in living the Christian life can be summarized as follows. First, I don't think we can ever move beyond the sheer power and significance of our spiritual "birthing" experiences, whether that is coming to faith in Christ, baptism, or the experience of the baptism of the Spirit. These formative and empowering experiences continue to be the basic building blocks of the spiritual life. Our task is to continue to reappropriate these significant encounters with the Holy One. Part of the task of the church is to help us in this process through its sacramental life—but whether the church does this well is a question I won't pursue here.

Second, any experiences that we have had of a visionary nature, divine healing, or other direct encounters with God must be seen as undeserved blessings and surprises in the journey of faith. They carry no significance in terms of status, and they should not be seen as marks of maturity. Rather, they are signs of the grace and goodness of God.

Third, the Christian life is not lived on the basis of accumulated goodness. There is no progress report or balance sheet. There is simply the daily bread of God's maintenance and provision in our daily lives. Our mantra is undeserved grace, not human achievement. This, however, does not exclude the fact that we are to appropriate and steward what God gives us. Our relationship with God is not marked by a passive waiting for God to act, but an active seeking of God.

Within this framework of God's ongoing faithfulness and care and the gift of the sustaining Spirit, we are called to live all the dimensions of life in the context of our family, church, work, and participation in the wider society. This calling brings both blessings and challenges.

One challenge is that even though we are "special" in the grace of Christ—and *all* are special in that grace, whether or not they embrace it—this grace does not cocoon us from life's difficulties. We will be affected by our own wrongdoing, the worldliness of the world, and all that life throws at us in terms of disasters, misfortunes, disease, and aging. We remain *creatures* in the grace of God, and thus we continue to experience all of life's realities. Grace does not turn us into angels, nor are we especially sheltered. We should remember that Christ was crucified as a common criminal, Christians were thrown to the lions, Christians ended up in the Soviet gulag, and Archbishop Oscar Romero was gunned down while serving Holy Communion.

At this point, we should ask the following question: If Christians are not protected in special ways, what does the grace of Christ mean? The short answer may lead us to the heartbeat of the whole Christian journey: the Christian life is not about special status and benefits, but who and what you love. This will give you both joy and heartache, for such is the nature of love.

Afterword

To make that more specific, we note that the Christian life is about entering into a transformative relationship with God through Christ in the Spirit. This relationship reorients us to become more and more like Christ and more and more engaged in God's concern for our world.

But living this way is a huge challenge, for it calls us to ongoing conversion—away from stubborn self-determination and futile self-sufficiency and towards greater humility and dependence on God's provision, sustenance, and direction for our lives. This means that we are called into a constant relationship with and attentiveness to the God who both nurtures us and sends us into the world.

This journey has nothing to do with progress or status, but rather an ongoing encounter with the One who is the very source of life, who is everywhere present in our world, and who calls us to intimacy and service.

This call invites us to build a hermitage of the heart. Such a hermitage is not a place, but a disposition. It is a tapestry of existence, a fabric of life, a way of being. It is who we are in both the inner recesses of our being and our engagement with others and the world.

Such a hermitage is both a gift and task. It is a gift from the ever-brooding Spirit, who brings to us the riches of Christ, and it is a task that we shepherd and steward as we engage those around us.

Simply put: receive and build such a hermitage!

Bibliography

Armstrong, R. J., and I. C. Brady, trans. *The Complete Works of Francis and Clare*. New York: Paulist, 1982.
Chittister, Joan. *The Monastery of the Heart: An Invitation to a Meaningful Life*. London: SPCK, 2011.
Crosby, Michael H. *Finding Francis, Following Christ*. Maryknoll, NY: Orbis, 2007.
Davies, Oliver, trans. *Celtic Spirituality*. New York: Paulist, 1999.
de Waal, Esther, ed. *The Celtic Vision: Prayers and Blessings from the Outer Hebrides*. Petersham, MA: St. Bede's, 1990.
de Waal, Esther. *Seeking God: The Way of St. Benedict*. Collegeville, MN: Liturgical, 2001
Delio, Ilia. *Franciscan Prayer*. Cincinnati, OH: St. Anthony Messenger, 2004.
Ellacuria, I., and J. Sobrino, eds. *Mysterium Liberationis*. Maryknoll, NY: Orbis, 1993.
Ellul, Jacques. *Hope in Time of Abandonment*. Translated by C. Edward Hopkin. New York: Seabury, 1973.
Friedmann, Robert. *The Theology of Anabaptism: An Interpretation*. Scottdale, PA: Herald, 1973.
Fry, Timothy, ed. *The Rule of Saint Benedict*. New York: Vintage, 1998.
Ganss, George E., ed. *Ignatius of Loyola: The Spiritual Exercises and Selected Works*. New York: Paulist, 1991.
Gorospe, Athena E., and Charles R. Ringma, eds. *How Long, O Lord? The Challenge and Promise of Reconciliation and Peace*. Carlisle, UK: Langham Global Library, 2018.
Grant-Thomson, Jeanette. *Jodie's Story: The Life of Jodie Cadman*. Vancouver, BC: Regent College Publishing, 2003.
Merton, Thomas. *The Wisdom of the Desert*. New York: New Directions, 1970.
Newell, J. Philip. *Listening for the Heartbeat of God: A Celtic Spirituality*. London: SPCK, 2008.
Northumbria Community. *Celtic Daily Prayer*. New York: HarperOne, 2002.
Ratcliffe, Susan, ed. *The Oxford Dictionary of Thematic Quotations*. Oxford: Oxford University Press, 2000.

Bibliography

Rees, Nigel, ed. *Brewer's Famous Quotations*. London: Weidenfeld & Nicolson, 2006.

Ricoeur, Paul. *Time and Narrative*. 3 vols. Chicago: University of Chicago Press, 1984–1988.

Ringma, Charles. "Franciscan Peacemaking: Making Connections with the Wider Christian Tradition." In *How Long, O Lord? The Challenge and Promise of Reconciliation and Peace,* edited by Athena E. Gorospe and Charles R. Ringma, 163–86. Carlisle, UK: Langham Global Library, 2018.

———. *Hear the Ancient Wisdom*. Eugene, OR: Cascade, 2013.

———. *Sabbath Time: A Hermitage Journey of Retreat, Return and Communion*. Carlisle, UK: Piquant, 2017.

Shenk, Wilbert R., ed. *Anabaptism and Mission*. Scottdale, PA: Herald, 1984.

Snyder, C. Arnold. *Following in the Footsteps of Christ: The Anabaptist Tradition*. Maryknoll, NY: Orbis, 2004.

Waddell, Helen. *The Desert Fathers*. New York: Vintage, 1998.

Ward, Benedicta, trans. *The Desert Fathers: Sayings of the Early Christian Monks*. London: Penguin, 2003.

Manufactured by Amazon.ca
Acheson, AB